RETIRE NOW!

Your Blueprint to Financial Freedom Through Property

GEORGE CHOY & SARAH CHOY

RETIRE NOW!

First published in the United Kingdom in 2019
by My Castle Property Training LLP
11 Abbott Way, Tenterden, Kent, TN30 7BZ, United Kingdom.
www.mycastlepublishing.com

This edition published in October 2019
© 2019 George David Choy & Sarah Jane Choy

George David Choy and Sarah Jane Choy have asserted their right to be identified as the authors of this work in accordance with sections 77 and 78 of the Copyright, Designs and Patents Act 1988.

All rights reserved. No part of this book may be reproduced by any means, electronic, mechanical, photocopying or otherwise, without the prior permission of the publisher.

British Library Cataloguing in Publication Data
A catalogue record is available for this book

Paperback ISBN: 9781093321845

MY CASTLE
PUBLISHING

My Castle Property Training LLP
11 Abbott Way, Tenterden, Kent, TN30 7BZ, United Kingdom.

Contents

Dedication 9

Foreword by Paul Smith, Touchstone Education 11

Secret bonus tools and resources 17

How to use this book 19

Chapter One: 23
Introduction 23

> You can't guarantee receiving a monthly income from your job 23
> About me—George Choy 31
> About me—Sarah Choy 32
> How we turned nothing into £1,760,000 33

Chapter Two 37
The RETIRE NOW! Blueprint 37

> How would you spend your days? 40

Chapter Three 43
Retirement Figure 43

Chapter Four 49
Expense Optimisation 49

> Improving your Credit Score 51
> Are you entitled to extra income? 56

Free Holidays 61
The day we realised were Financially Independent... 63
How to save over 1% of your expenses 67
Can you Retire Now? 69
What is your Net Worth? 72
Conspicuous consumption 73

Chapter Five 77
Thoughts & Dreams 77

What are Values? 78
Your voids 80
Identify your values 80
Design your Dream life 84
Establishing a wealthy mindset 89
A high income does not make you wealthy 90
RETIRE NOW! Declarations 93

Chapter Six 99
Income Producing Assets 99

Your home is bad for your wealth 102
Finding hidden money 105
Income streams 112
Courage Pot 114
How to hold your Assets—Company structures 115
Capital Allowances—Tax-Free Income 119
How to set up a company 121
Buy-to-Let (BTL) 123
Serviced Accommodation (SA) 143
Rent-to-Rent (R2R) 171
Commercial Property 185
Don't be a loser 207

Chapter Seven 209
Retirement Systemisation 209

Chapter Eight 229
Education... 229

Chapter Nine 237
Network 237

Chapter Ten 243
One's Purpose... 243

Chapter Eleven 247
Wellbeing 247

Chapter Twelve 265
Property Investing—what would we have done differently?... 265

Contact 269

DISCLAIMER

This book contains information on the subject matter it covers. The information is not advice and should not be treated as such.

You must not rely on the information in this book or the accompanying materials available for download as an alternative to financial, investment, legal, taxation, accountancy, or medical advice from an appropriately qualified professional. You should never delay seeking professional advice because of the information contained in this report.

You should always seek the advice of your doctor, physician and dietitian before beginning an exercise routine or changing your diet.

No warranty is made with respect to the accuracy or completeness of the information contained herein or in the accompanying materials available for download, and both the authors and My Castle Property Training LLP specifically disclaim any responsibility for liability, loss, or risk, personal or otherwise, which is incurred as a consequence, directly or indirectly of the use and application of any of the contents of this book or accompanying downloads.

Some of the links contained in this book or in the web pages or materials available for download may be affiliate links. This means that if you click on the link it will be tracked and it may generate a payment to the Author or Publisher. We believe this does not compromise the integrity of this book and materials for download, because with or without affiliate links the Author's would still recommend the same products or services.

This disclaimer will be governed by and construed in accordance with English law, and any disputes relating to this disclaimer will be subject to the exclusive jurisdiction of the courts of England and Wales.

Dedication

We would like to thank our parents, Margaret and David, and Linda and Brian for all the help they've given us over the years—particularly in our lowest moments.

We also thank Linda and Brian for many weekends helping out with decorating our properties in the early years, and for babysitting our children whilst we were on property courses.

Thanks to our property mentors Paul and Aniko Smith at Touchstone Education, for believing in us, and stoking our fire.

Thanks to all of our property friends for their ongoing support—there's too many to mention. It's always good catching up with people who understand what we're doing, and who we can rely on.

Thank you,

George & Sarah

Foreword by Paul Smith, Touchstone Education

As the owner of one of the largest property training companies in the UK—I've met a lot of people trying to improve their lives through property.

I've known George and Sarah for fifteen months. They are two of the most inspirational people that I've had the pleasure to mentor. If you've got the internet, it's hard to miss them. These aren't just my thoughts. Whenever I look at what people are commenting about them online, there's a stream of people thanking them for sharing their journey and telling them what an inspiration they are to other property investors.

Just before I met them—one of the things they did to raise funds for property investing and to pay for mentorship, was to sell their home. I'm not aware of my course making someone homeless before…it was a first!

George told me that for the last two months, Facebook produced a video showing that I was his closest friend…so not only did I make them homeless, but they now have no friends except me :-)

In the short time I've known them, they've bought Commercial Property, converted Buy-to-Lets into Serviced Accommodation, done a Joint Venture on a Commercial to Residential Conversion, set up companies, written a book and are now Mentors.

George and Sarah are HUGE action takers. They are willing to do things that people think are too hard or complex. So, if you give them a challenge, they will be one of the few people to make it happen.

They are financially free and have a life most people dream of having. Some of their passions are going to the gym, spa and cinema during the day whilst their two young children are at school…and everyone else is at work. They now get to CHOOSE how to fill their time.

It was a privilege to be asked to write the Foreword. *RETIRE NOW!* is the culmination of their 15 years in property, and time spent researching and devising a step-by-step system to becoming financially free.

They have a unique approach of attempting to only work one hour a month on their property business and have at last put pen to paper to share their knowledge with others.

They wrote this book in a detailed, methodical and interactive way…interspersed with their infectious humour. If you've ever watched one of their vlogs, you'll know what I mean!

> Foreword by Paul Smith,
> Touchstone Education

This book has the power to transform lives. I look forward to watching where their property journey takes them next.

Paul Smith

Touchstone Education

This page has been intentionally left blank

Foreword by Paul Smith,
Touchstone Education

This page has been intentionally left blank

This page has been intentionally left blank

Secret bonus tools and resources

The value we've provided doesn't stop with this book.

We've put together **secret bonus resources**, designed to go hand in hand with this book, to help you get results and save you time. These bonuses are exclusively for you, as a reader of this book. We'll signpost in the book when you need to reference the resource page.

1. Visit this link to register and get the password:
mycastleproperty.co.uk/rnpass

2. The password protected bonus link:

mycastleproperty.co.uk/retirenowbonus

Write your password here: *happy Life 39*
(it is all in lower case and includes spaces)

Please do me a favour and keep the link our little secret. You can submit suggestions for the book on the bonus webpage.

How to use this book

Congratulations for buying this book. You are on the verge of changing your life, forever.

This is the book that we wish we'd had 15 years ago. We've made so many mistakes over the years. We've bought properties we shouldn't have…we've bought in locations we shouldn't, and yet somehow, we've still come out on top, despite all these shortcomings.

It just goes to show you—**property mistakes are like a bad haircut…they grow out in the end.**

We retired when Sarah turned 39—that was amazing, and way beyond everyone else around us…who were still going to work, every single day. We still pinch ourselves when we are at a vineyard, spa or the cinema during the day when our children are at school—or even being able to attend one of their class assemblies, where George will be one of the few dads that could make it.

Now if we'd known…if we'd had the knowledge that we have now…the property that we have would be paying at least double or triple our current income. Moreover, we could have retired within one year during our twenties. You don't need as much property as we have—we were inefficient with our funds in the past.

I wish we'd read the information contained in this book before we'd even considered buying our own home or investing in property. I never realised that it was possible to create a property business with none of your own money.

Not only that, but we know many, many property investors…and **very few of them are financially free**—and it's all because they don't know about the wealth systems that you need in order to become financially free. So, whilst they own property, they don't know how to correctly apply the systems around it, in order to retire.

Consequently, this book is for those people with no property experience…one or two properties…or a large property portfolio. Wherever you are on your journey, this book will help you to retire now.

This book is also a workbook—it's meant to be written on. You'll be filling out your answers to exercises as you read. Practicing is one of the best ways to learn and retain information.

This book should be read sequentially—as a step-by-step process to becoming financially free. If you jump ahead you might miss a critical step.

In addition, it's really useful to have the *RETIRE NOW!* Resources web page open at the same time on your phone or computer, so you can watch videos, click on links, and download useful documents whilst you follow along with the text.

All right, buckle up, we're going to challenge and shake up your view of the world—let's get started…

George & Sarah

CHAPTER ONE:
Introduction

You can't guarantee receiving a monthly income from your job.

Do you know any companies that have gone bankrupt or into administration?

There are many global brands that nobody would have thought this would ever happen to, in the financial services, airlines and retail industries.

And what happens to their employees? Do you know anyone that has ever been made redundant?

Alternatively, do you know anyone that has ever been on maternity leave?

If so, then you might be aware that after 6 weeks of maternity leave you will only receive £148.68 per week…it's difficult to live on that…and after 39 weeks you receive zero income! If you've been on a high earning salary, then going on maternity leave will be a shock to your finances if you have no passive income to rely on.

Do you know anyone that had to stop working because they were physically or mentally sick?

I know people where the stress of their job was so great, that they had a nervous breakdown and were never able to come back to work again. They had no additional income to fall back on.

I know people who've had a heart attack, or broken their leg, which meant they were not able to work while they recovered…and **their income vanished.**

According to a report published by Dell Technologies, 85% of the jobs that will exist in 2030, haven't been invented yet. And with the increase in the use of automation, you can already see that people are starting to get replaced.

For example, there are now trucks that drive themselves in the USA—how long before taxis are automated? There are more automated checkouts in supermarkets. Bank branches are closing, as jobs are automated. Amazon is testing out drones to deliver parcels. The whole job market is changing—the jobs we know today are slowly disappearing.

This book is what we've learned over fifteen years of property investing, and two years of intense research into how to become financially free.

We had property…but weren't financially free. We just didn't know how to make that happen. It just seemed like a pot of gold at the end of the rainbow, one that we might never reach.

The aims of this book are to make you Financially Free as soon as possible. That could take a couple of days, a few months, a year, or more. We will be covering how to:

- Optimise your expenses—many of these things are just simple switches that will make a huge increase to the amount of money you will have left over each month.

- Calculate the income needed for you to retire. You may already have a number in mind…we will help you to validate that.

- You will be able to estimate when you can stop working. And the answer could be surprising— you might find that you are very close. Certainly, when we ran through this process, we suddenly discovered that we were already financially free…we just didn't know it.

- Help you to change from a "Poor" person's mindset into a "Wealthy" person's mindset. This is absolutely critical. If you think "poor" you will make poor decisions every day—you need to change to a "wealthy" mindset. **This one thing held back my financial freedom for decade**s and is the sticking point for most people.

- Identify hidden money. When you ask people why

they haven't invested in property, a lot of people give the excuse that they don't have any money. We show you where you can find money.

- You then can spend some time deciding what you will do with your life when you become financially free. We went through a period of self-gratification…and we were completely aimless…we didn't know how we wanted to spend the rest of our lives. So, it's good to plan this out now, so you can focus all your efforts towards that goal and achieve it much faster.

- The next pages are for your 7 day, 1 month, 3 month and 1 year RETIRE NOW! Action Plans. To increase your chance of success, I recommend you **fill out your plans as you read through the pages of this book.**

If you need more space to write you can download A4 versions of the action plans by visiting the RETIRE NOW! Bonus page at **mycastleproperty.co.uk/retirenowbonus**

If you don't have the password, then go back to the *Secret Bonus Tools and Resources* chapter earlier in the book.

Introduction

RETIRE NOW! Action Plan
I commit to doing the following **within 7 days**
By date: **20**/10/19

① Go through 3 months worth of bank Statements + see what we spend.

② Find good images of THE House. Parts of the house - Pool, Tennis Court Trampoline - in the ground!? Dance Studio Meditation space. Walled Victorian garden. Our own organic Veg. Victorian greenhouse for Veg + fruit. Chickens, Gardener + Cook onsite, with family that our kids love. Within 20 mins drive of fabulous school. Space/horse for John + Rooms for guests/Family Great offices for us both, Coaching Room.

③ Key Castle Property Guaranty Introduce myself + Add Photo Why do I want to be financially free?

④ Check Credit score pg 51-52

⑤ Make sure everything is Registered for Carteeple.

27

RETIRE NOW! Action Plan
I commit to doing the following **within 1 month**
By date: 10/11/19

✳ Put everything on DD. Make sure I don't pay anything late again. This might take a bit of time
No 0% Cards for Balance Transfers?

How much credit is available to me, how much am I using? Ideal Range is 20-30%

Reduce credit card debt - Close M+S card
Increase limits on cards? in 4 months →

Check if we're entitled to any benefits
If so put into a savings account + use it to invest in property

Get Retire Now Spreadsheet pg 59
Do expenses

RETIRE NOW! Action Plan
I commit to doing the following **within 3 months**
By date: _____

RETIRE NOW! Action Plan
I commit to doing the following **within 1 year**
By date: _____

About me—George Choy

I've been a property landlord for fifteen years, and together with Sarah, we have a property portfolio worth over £1,760,000.

Our property portfolio includes Commercial Property, Serviced Accommodation and Buy-to-Lets. We have also Joint Ventured on Commercial Conversions and raised Private Finance.

I've spent nineteen years in business and credit card, insurance, and media marketing. I've got an MBA, a diploma in marketing, a degree in computer science (so I love systems and analysing property deals.) One of my other passions is health and fitness, so I also became a qualified Personal Trainer.

About me—Sarah Choy

I've also been a landlord for fifteen years, as George and I started the business together.

I worked in an Estate Agency and Lettings Agency for 3½ years, so I have a lot of knowledge about buying and selling houses.

I ran a design and marketing agency for fifteen years, as I'm the creative one in the relationship.

Like George, one of my values is health and fitness. I have a degree in biochemistry, and I'm also a qualified Nutritional Consultant.

How we turned nothing into £1,760,000

> *"Someone's sitting in the shade today because someone planted a tree a long time ago."*
>
> —WARREN BUFFETT

We started with nothing! So, if you don't have any money, then great—you can start exactly where we started.

Sarah's parents gave us £5,000 as a wedding present. We'd been together for six years, but I hadn't set a date to get married. So, this was a big hint for me to "pull my finger out!"

What to spend it on? Should we go out and blow that £5,000 on a nice holiday…

No, what we did was buy a very small starter home. It was an end of terrace workman's cottage, built with chart stone. It was very charming and situated in a relatively expensive village in Surrey.

It was very small. It had one double bedroom and a box room that we used as an office. Downstairs there was only enough room for a two-seater sofa and a TV. It was so small…you could almost get up the stairs in one leap. The bus stopped right outside our bedroom window, so we put up thick net curtains, so people couldn't see us naked!

We bought it for £97,000 (using the £5,000 as a deposit), and we sold it two years later for £125,000. A profit of £28,000.

We didn't realise it at the time, but **this was the start of using other people's money** to build a property empire.

After selling our first home, we moved to a town house in a cheaper area—which meant we could have a larger property. As that went up in value, we remortgaged it to withdraw £68,000 for Buy-To-Let properties—this was the start of our investment business. We divided that money up into deposits for four houses.

Unfortunately, we bought just a couple of years before the peak of the housing market crash. But the thing about property is…as long as you are investing for the long term and your properties are making good monthly cashflow, then it doesn't matter when the housing market dips. All that matters is how much money you are getting in the bank every month.

We made the mistake of buying four properties at exactly the same time. It hit our bank account hard, as they were all vacant and we had to start paying the mortgages.

A few years later, the housing market predictably rose again.

Then we carried on saving, raised some private finance and bought three more properties.

We sold our home and bought a lovely converted barn. It was single-story, so we did a loft conversion to build two more bedrooms.

Our property portfolio was doing well, so we downshifted, and I qualified to become a Personal Trainer, and Sarah trained to become a Nutritional Consultant. We only worked a couple of hours a day.

Then we started researching how to become financially free, and how to systemise our lives so we could retire. We developed systems to help us do it—which we've refined in this book. When Sarah was 39 we suddenly realised… "wait a minute, we can RETIRE NOW!"

It was a shock. We thought we had to continue working, but just didn't realise we could stop at any time. So that became the point when we retired.

We stopped promoting the Personal Training business but carried on working out our existing clients—as they had become our closest friends. I was only working about three hours a day…but it didn't feel like work to me as it was so much fun. We sat back and relaxed in-between.

After a while, we thought to ourselves "Why retire on what we have now? What if we wanted to take our property business to the next level?"

We then realised we were are sitting on a ton of cash stuck in our home. "If we sold our house, we could use the cash to buy investment properties, and then rent a house with the income…we would still have money left over."

So, we sold our "forever" home, making over £300,000 profit. We used the cash to buy a commercial property and did a Joint Venture on a commercial conversion.

That brings us up to today…starting with nothing, and turning £5,000 into 8 properties worth over £1,760,000, and only needing to work one hour per month. We plan to increase our portfolio to at least £2.6 million.

We did it the hard way and learned from lot of mistakes. If you put in the work, you can do it much quicker than us and retire in a year or less. Others have done it.

CHAPTER TWO

The RETIRE NOW! Blueprint

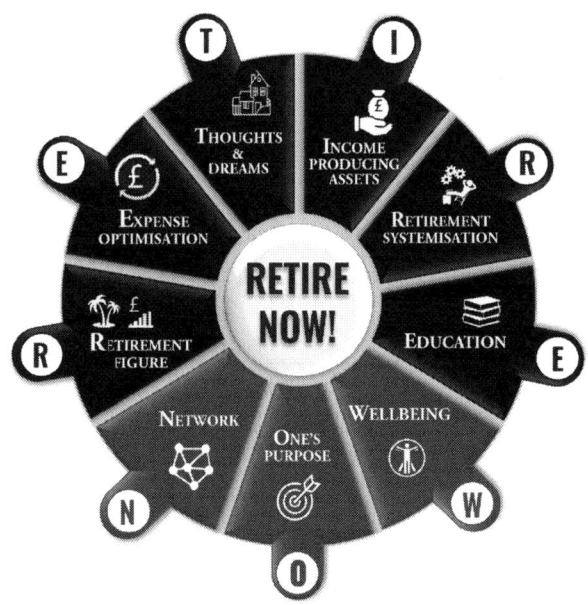

This is the system we developed to become financially free. **Even if you already have property**, this can suddenly make you realise you can retire now.

Download the RETIRE NOW! Blueprint model on the RETIRE NOW! bonus page
mycastleproperty.co.uk/retirenowbonus

- *Retirement Figure:* You will work out how much money you need to retire—at low, medium and high levels. Once you've put the rest of the blueprint model in place, you may find that this figure is lower than you first thought.

- *Expense Optimisation:* When we went through this exercise, we increased our monthly cash flow by £1,000 per month! Imagine if I gave you a cheque for £12,000 right now? What difference would that make to your life? Could you retire already, or work less days? We will show you how to do it, and how to find hidden money.

- *Thoughts and Dreams:* This is an area that I've really struggled with over the years. It's about how to change your mindset. **The biggest stumbling block to becoming financially free…is you.** You are the barrier—you are the thing standing in the way of your financial freedom. We are going to help you to change your mindset from a "poor" mindset, to a "wealthy" mindset.
And we're also going to help you to identify your values—so you can design your dream life, and focus your energy on achieving it.

- *Income Producing Assets:* there are many strategies, but we will focus on a few that can get you financially free. These are Buy-to-Lets, Serviced Accommodation, Rent-to-Rent and Commercial Property.

We will also go through how you might want to structure your companies, and how you can save tax.

- *Retirement Systemisation:* the whole point of being financially free is that you don't actually need to do any work. We know property investors that are working all day long—they are taking calls at weekends and on holidays...they are cleaning properties...painting...showing tenants around properties...in essence, doing lots of low paid tasks.

   What if you are sick? What if you become injured and can't work? Your business falls down. We will show you how to construct your business to get out of this trap. Sarah and I could go on holiday for a month or a year and not need to do anything. If one of us is sick, it's not a problem.

- *Education:* Dr John Demartini says *"The individuals who invest in their education are buying opportunities."* If we'd had the correct knowledge of property and systems when we started, we could have retired in our twenties. Sure, we are degree educated, but we didn't have the right property knowledge. Since then, we've spent over £45,000 on property and self-improvement courses. We see education as a never-ending experience—something we must never stop doing. Imagine implementing one small thing in your property portfolio that compounds over the years to provide huge gains.

- *Network:* Your network is your net worth. In here are the steps you can take to improve the value of your network. In your network there will be many things such as knowledge, money and deals—this will help you.

- *One's Purpose:* When you no longer have to work anymore and decide to 'retire'…if you don't have a plan in place, you are like a ship without a compass—drifting at sea. Consequently, you should work out what your purpose is in life.

- *Wellbeing:* If you don't have your health, then you don't have a business. Here we give you the top tips from the clients we helped in our Personal Training business. We will show you the simple things you can do to transform your health and look good.

How would you spend your days?

What will you do with yourself when you are Financially Free and don't need to work? **You can choose** how to spend your time.

When we first discovered we were Financially Free and retired, we would get up…take our kids to school…go to the spa to exercise and have a massage, then some lunch, before putting on our robes to read whilst drinking cups of green tea and water in the relaxation room. Later we picked up our children on the way home. That's typically how we spent our days for six months…

Exercise 1:
<u>Now close your eyes and spend a couple of minutes imagining your perfect day unfolding…from waking up…breakfast…lunch…dinner…the evening…imagine what you could be doing every day for the rest of your life.</u>

<u>We visualise every day, during our morning meditation. If you can imagine it, you can make it a reality.</u>

Wake up together with Al. Have an alarm playing Its a brand new day Everytimes Lights that slowly come on with alarm Al + me get exercise gear on + go to our dance studio / gym Mirrored walls. Warm comfy. Drink our water Do dance / exercise / yoga / 2 seperate spaces to work out in. Then Meditate, shower, dress. eat breakfasts prepared by our cook the night before. The boys get up + we do some fun dance wake up Routine with them after 5 mins silence. Healthy brekkey for them. Some reading + home work. Get them dressed for day to their fantastic school, which they both <u>love</u>

RETIRE NOW!

We both drive them to school in my gorgeous red hybrid car. Then Al + me go to see one of our new properties which is almost ready for a national brand to move into. The upstairs is 2 SH units we in Shrewsbury. Then we head to the shops to buy a last few things for our selves for our up coming holiday with the boys. We'll be going first class - no waiting, no queueing.

We go for lunch in Shrewsbury + head back home. We are having the guest lodge done up for John to come + stay.

When we're home, we check out some new properties with our commercial storage and make an appointment to see our tomorrow.

The next day I am booked for body wrap nails, eyelashes, eyebrows + toes for my hols.

Al + me look at each other in our beautiful new home with such love, admiration + pride at what we've done.

We've cleared all our C cards all our debts families debts. Helped them get into property + out of work.

I have a quick chat with cook about dinner + then head out to collect the boys. Indie has won a prize for his story + Noah has won a swimming competition. My heart

CHAPTER THREE

Retirement Figure

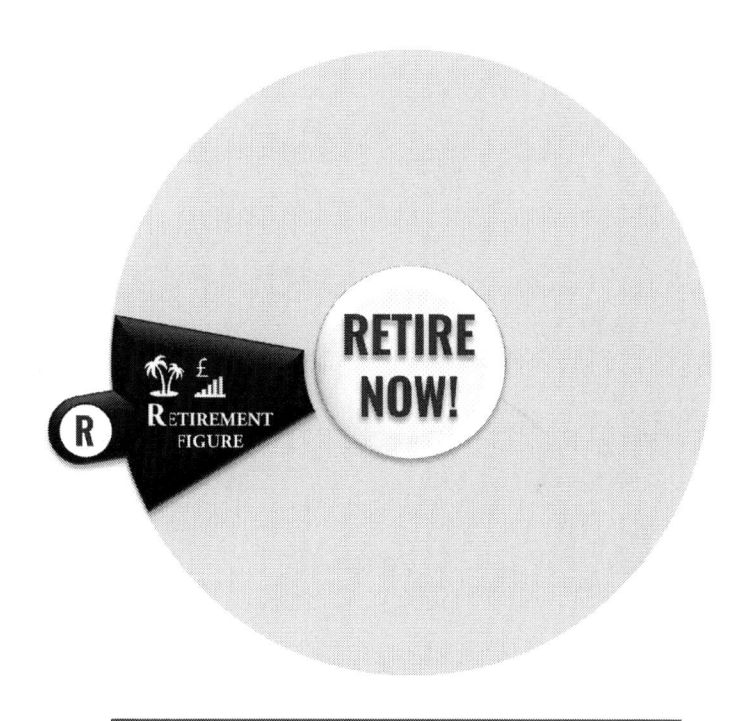

"If you think being an entrepreneur is risky, try working for someone else for 40 years and living off social security."

—WARREN BUFFETT

is bursting with pride,
The boys love their new home. and Now
can finally have a dog!

When we wrote this book, the UK State Pension was £168.60 per week / £675 per month. Looking at how much you spend now…could you survive on that little money? Or do you need more?

According to *LV= State of Retirement report 2017*, the average amount people hold in their personal pension pot is £71,342. That is only the average—and there are plenty of people with £1 million in their pot, and most with a lot less than the average, or none at all.

When the majority of people turn 65, they take out an annuity, which pays you an income for life. What I dislike about annuities is that the returns are lower than property investing, and it usually disappears when you die. That's a lot of money to lose, and nothing to pass to your children and future generations.

For example, let's say you have £100,000 in your pension pot—that could pay you a whopping £3,000 a year! Not exactly exciting. Who could live on that? It would take 33 years just for you to get back what you invested.

Consequently, if you retire at 65 and are in good enough health to reach 98 years old, then you will break even at that point—but of course inflation will have eroded its value. But as the average life expectancy is currently 81 years old, the annuity companies are counting on you dying before you get your money back.

Retirement Figure

Exercise 2:
My personal pension pot is worth: £ _0_
Multiply by 3% to get what you might receive per year:
£_____

÷ by 12 to get what it will pay you per month:
£_____

Add together the monthly income from the state pension £675 plus your personal pension
£_____

That's how much you will have to live on. Of course, the retirement date is gradually being extended—a think tank recently recommended extending it to 75 years…probably because there's a huge deficit in the pension fund—I wonder if there will even be a state pension by the time we reach that age? Not good news for those people counting on it as their only source of income.

Let me ask you a question…would you like to **retire on more money per month**, than you have now? And would you like the amount of **money to go up every year**, instead of down? You will actually get richer, the older you get.

And what if your pension pot could be inherited by future generations. Now wouldn't that be a nicer scenario? Well that's what can happen when you transfer your personal pension into a SIPP or SSAS—you can put Commercial property into it and receive the rent as income. After all that's one of the things that pension companies invest in. We will be covering SIPP and SSAS in *Chapter Six: Income Producing Assets*.

> "A wealthy person is simply someone who has learned how to make money when they're not working."
>
> –ROBERT KIYOSAKI

I love that quote from Robert Kiyosaki—author of the book *Rich Dad, Poor Dad*. It simply means you need to invest in assets that make money while you sleep…that is the only way to become truly financially free.

Sarah and I recommend people set three levels of financial freedom:

Level 1: Financial Independence
This covers all your basic living expenses, but doesn't cover holidays, big purchases or other luxuries. It's just basic living—but you could quit your job at this level (if you want to).

Level 2: Financial Freedom
This includes luxury holidays, prestige cars (the "good life").

Level 3: Financial Abundance
This is when you no longer worry about money and can do whatever you want.

Exercise 3:

Write down your three levels, so you have targets to aim for…and most importantly, so you'll know you could give up your job when you hit level 1—if you want to.

My financial freedom targets:

> Level 1: Financial Independence
> £_____ per month
>
>
> Level 2: Financial Freedom
> £_____ per month
>
>
> Level 3: Financial Abundance
> £_____ per month

I want to get up on a wet Friday and be able to have looked at the forecast the night before. Packed our bags + booked to fly somewhere warm. Italy, Spain, Sth of France. Tell the boys they're not going to school, the car is packed (by alfred!)
He'll drive us to the Airport and we can go for a week! (or 2)

CHAPTER FOUR
Expense Optimisation

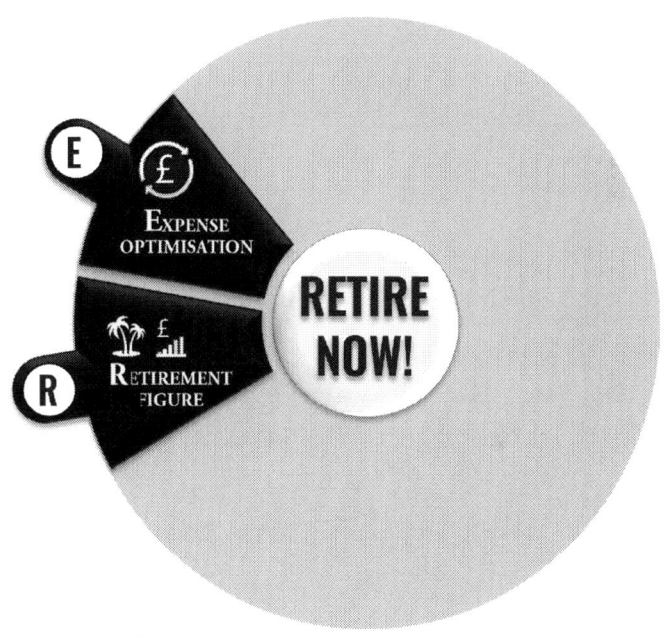

Exercise 4:
    I will turn 65 in __15__ years.

    If I have to work until then, this is what my life will be like in the meantime…

I won't have the time I want to spend with Alan or the kids. We will have less holidays. Alan is always on the phone or laptop. Snaps at the kids. Not enough time to play with the boys

RETIRE NOW!

Spending too much time making ends meet.

Are you happy with that?
Would you like to be free sooner?

Great! Read on…

We retired when Sarah turned 39 years old. YOU are the biggest barrier to becoming financially free. I want you to show your commitment by taking action.

Exercise 5:
Go onto Facebook. If you don't already have a personal account, then go ahead and sign up—it's free.

Search for the group *My Castle Property community* and Join it.

Write a post:
- Add a photo of yourself.
- Introduce yourself.
- Tell people why you want to commit to becoming financially free and what difference it will make to your life.

Congratulations. Studies show that **you are more likely to achieve declarations you have made public**. You've just increased your probability of success. If you are feeling really brave post it on your timeline as well—this will supercharge your motivation! Include the hashtag #retirenowblueprint

Improving your Credit Score

It doesn't matter whether you earn £12,000 a year, or one billion per year—everybody needs mortgages and lending in order to become really successful in property investing. And you need to maintain and improve your credit score in order to get lending in the first place.

By regularly monitoring your credit score, you will be aware when your score starts to drop, so you can take steps to improve it. Every time you apply for a credit card, mortgage, loan or mobile phone, those companies will check with their favourite credit-referencing agency.

There are 3 main agencies that companies check against: Experian, Equifax and CallCredit. If one of them has an error that gives you a poor credit score, then you could get declined for a mortgage by one company and accepted by another who uses a different agency. I regularly check all three reports and recommend you do too.

Exercise 6:

> Check your credit score. There are lots of paid subscriptions, but I recommend you sign up for a free account at all three of the following:
>
> *1. Credit Club*
> moneysavingexpert.com/creditclub

This shows the data held on you by Experian. They also email you when your score has changed.

2. ClearScore
clearscore.com
Data from Equifax.

3. Credit karma
creditkarma.co.uk
Data from Callcredit.

You will probably find that your score is better or worse on each provider. If one is worse than the others, then look deeper to discover whether something is incorrect.

Tips on raising your credit score:

- According to Clear Score, 38% of people find mistakes on their credit report when they first check it. Therefore, you should check it thoroughly the first time. For example, perhaps you paid off a debt, but it is incorrectly showing as outstanding.

- If you have credit cards, store cards, or other accounts that are open, but you don't use them, then close them down.

- Be wary of becoming financially linked to anyone with a poor credit score. Keep that in mind if you decide to open a company with someone. If you get a mortgage or credit card with another person, then their credit score can impact yours. So be very careful.

- **Make sure you are on the electoral roll.** I've met many people who have been declined for mortgages, because they didn't think this was important—they weren't registered at all. Also make sure that all forms of validating your identity are at the same address. Whenever you apply for something like a credit card, or a mobile phone, they validate against the electoral roll to check whether you live where you say you do. If they don't match, then you will get declined. Applying for products just after you have moved to a new house can be a problem, as records don't match. It's preferential to stay in the same home for at least one year.

- **You must, must, must, pay all your mortgages, credit cards and utility bills on time.** Even forgetting to pay your mobile phone bill on time will negatively impact your credit score, and it could last for many years.

- Don't put yourself in the situation where you get a CCJ, IVA, bankruptcy or any other debt related order—that will cause you huge problems in getting mortgages and loans in the future. If this has already happened, then take steps to improve your credit file. There are still property strategies you can do such as Rent to Rent (covered later), that don't require a good credit score (providing you will still be eligible to sign up for utilities such as water, gas, electricity, etc.).

- Never withdraw cash on a credit card or get a pay day loan. Lenders view this as bad money management.

- Getting a product on 0% finance, or 0% balance transfer cards can negatively impact your credit score as it can also indicate bad money management, and some of these products are seen by lenders as less regulated and therefore you are riskier.

- Don't apply for multiple products at the same time—it makes it look like you are desperate for cash, so your score will go down. Space them out. Apply for a mobile phone, and then wait a week or two before applying for a credit card or mortgage.

Don't get into bad debt

If you are only paying off the minimum balance on your credit cards, or you take out payday loans, then you need to set yourself some no spending weeks, so you can pay off all those debts as fast as possible and never get into the situation again.

I used to work for a credit card company. I can tell you

that these types of loan facilities are some of the highest APRs in the industry and will keep you poor.

I often meet people who don't even have £100 in savings and they try to borrow from friends just to make it through the month. Then I hear they are going on holiday abroad next month, or they just bought a wide screen TV…bad cashflow management will make them poor forever. They need to stop spending, and only use debt for income producing assets.

One more tip: Total credit and credit utilisation

You need to have your own credit, not someone else's.

Make sure you are the main or only account holder on a credit card—being an additional or supplementary card doesn't count. Being the main person means that you are responsible for the credit—so if your wife only has one of your additional cards, then she does not have any of that credit in her name. No credit = less creditworthy.

It is better to apply for credit cards separately, so you can each build the amount of credit you have available. If you don't have much credit available, then it becomes harder to get loans and mortgages—so being 100% debt free can be problem.

Exercise 7:

> Take a look at your credit report to find out how much credit you have available to you, and how much you are utilising. An ideal range is 20-30%.

For example, if you have £10,000 of credit and your balance is £3,000 then your credit utilisation is 30%.

However, if you reach 50% credit utilisation then it will have a major negative impact on your credit score…that is why it is useful to increase the amount of credit available to you. You can usually request a credit limit increase every 4-6 months. However, some credit cards aimed at building credit scores will do this automatically.

If you are not the main account holder, then write it on your action plan for the next 7 days…but **don't apply for a credit card just yet**, as there is a specific type of card we will be recommending later in this section.

Are you entitled to extra income?

Let me ask you a question…have you ever paid tax?

If you have, then know this…your tax pays for benefits that may be due to you. **You are entitled to this**. This is passive income. This is owed to you. Here are some common ones.

Child benefit: If you have children, which many of us do, then you are entitled to £89.70 per month for one child, or £149 per month for two children. However, once one of you earns over £50,000 per year then you lose the benefit. Do you meet these criteria? Have you claimed?

Disability benefit: perhaps you look after a disabled or autistic child? You could be earning up to £645 a month.

Carers allowance: do you care for a disabled person for 35 hours a week? Many people have their elderly mother or partner living with them. You could be entitled to £398 a month. My mother looked after my dad when he required full-time nursing after being diagnosed with Parkinson's.

Attendance allowance: what if you need a carer for yourself? You could receive £287 a month. Or if you are caring for your relative, then they can claim that.

These amounts will vary according to your personal circumstances.

Exercise 8:

> Check whether you are entitled to any benefits. There may be free money that your tax has paid for. You are entitled to this, so don't be proud. Use it for property investing.
>
> England
> gov.uk/browse/benefits
>
> Scotland
> mygov.scot/benefits
>
> I've discovered I'm entitled to the following benefits and monthly amounts:

_____

_____

_____

_____

_____

A word of warning…as your circumstances change in the future, your benefits may reduce or disappear (such as your child turning 16 years old or earning above the income thresholds).

So, don't spend benefit money—make sure you put it into a savings account and use it to invest in property. We will cover property strategies later in the *Income Producing Assets* section.

> "What gets measured gets managed"
>
> —PETER DRUCKER
> THE FATHER OF MANAGEMENT THEORY

Exercise 9: Calculate your personal expenses

This is a critical step—if you skip it you will never know when you become financially free. Not only that, but we are about to **save you thousands of pounds…**

Don't guess your expenses. Get out your last three

months of personal expenses—bank statements, credit cards, etc.

Categorise your expenditure. If you have expenses such as utility bills that are paid once a quarter, then divide them by 3 to get a monthly figure. If you have annual expenses such as insurance, then divide those by 12 to get the monthly amount. It should take you about 40 minutes.

Once you've done that for 3 months, then total up the months and divide by 3, to get your 3-month average.

Example categories are listed below. Please feel free to add further categories.

> You can download an expense optimisation spreadsheet by visiting the RETIRE NOW! Bonus page mycastleproperty.co.uk/retirenowbonus

Gas £ — /month
Electricity £ 109
Wastewater £ —
Water £ 32
Council tax £ 150
Mortgage or rent £ 400
Landline £ —
Internet £ —
Mobiles £ — *business*
Garden waste/recycling collection £ —

RETIRE NOW!

TV licence £ —

Cars (purchase price divided by years kept/lease) £ 48
Car 1 insurance £ 36
Car 1 Tax £ _____
Car 1 Servicing £ _____
Car 2 insurance £ _____
Car 2 Tax £ _____
Car 2 Servicing £ _____
Petrol £ _____ Business
Repairs £ 11

Haircuts £ 13
Beauty treatments £ 10
Chiropractor etc. £ 43
Dentist £ 5
Optician/Glasses £ 22

Food £ 756
Supplements £ —
Meals out £ 93

Kids clubs £ —
Kids parties/presents £ 48
Childcare £ —

Pet insurance £ —
Life insurance £ 21
Health insurance £ 55
House maintenance contract £ —

The more times you say it, the more times your mind will believe and make it happen. It can also be helpful to look at yourself in the mirror whilst you say it.

The day we realised were Financially Independent

We optimised our expenses...

By switching providers and cancelling things we rarely used, we saved £1,000 per month and realised we were financially free and just didn't know it.

Imagine someone handing you £12,000 per year in cash, just for doing a little bit of work on the phone and internet right now. It's bonkers not to do it.

And before you think we were living like monks, we were still going to restaurants, driving a £42,000 Land Rover Discovery and living in a house worth nearly £700,000. Some of the swaps we made follow below. **We were able to retire in a matter of days.**

TV

After analysing our expenses, we cancelled our £45 a month Sky Satellite TV subscription (which we'd never thought we could be without) and started a Netflix account at only £8.99 a month. We couldn't be happier...and there were no adverts to watch.

Mobile Phone

We switched from £45 a month mobile phone contract with Vodafone, to EE, and paid only £25 a month with more data, more texts and free calls. We got a much better deal at nearly half the price. We moved two mobiles, so we saved £40 per month.

Groceries

We get most of our grocery shopping delivered to our house. We find it so convenient ordering online. We had been using Ocado for many years and never thought we would ever switch. Well, we put a basket of goods from our shopping over the last month into Tesco online and found we could save £200 a month for the same goods! Crazy.

Not only that, but if you switched to eating only Vegan whole food, **you can halve your grocery shopping bill** again and save hundreds more per month. Natural whole Vegan food is soooooo much cheaper. For example, a can of beans or lentils costs only 50 pence, versus £1.50 for a chicken breast. You could even decide to go "meatless" just a couple of days a week, if you don't feel you can go all in.

Utilities and Insurance

We moved our gas and electricity and fixed it for 2 years using uSwitch.com

We changed our boiler cover provider, house insurance, and car insurance.

We called BT to tell them we were thinking about cancelling and renegotiated the price of our phone package.

We cancelled several magazine subscriptions, and memberships that we weren't finding valuable.

Second Car

This was a huge saving. **We were only using our second car once every two weeks,** so we sold it. Say goodbye to those extra insurance costs, road tax, servicing, maintenance and the largest cost…depreciation. We worked out we were losing hundreds of pounds per month.

Instead we hired a driver for those few pickups from the train station each month. We sold it on autotrader.co.uk, which was surprisingly simple. You can also check the second-hand value of your car on the site.

Ebay or Facebook Marketplace

Declutter. A tidy house is a tidy mind.

Sell all the high value items that you've been keeping "just in case" and have not used in the last 12 months. I had a lot of power tools that I'd never, or rarely used.

Exercise 10: Optimise your expenses

> Go through all the expenses you identified, and decide for each one:
> 1. Whether you actually use them enough to

make them worthwhile, or should cancel them instead?

2. If you do need them, then research whether you can get them cheaper. You may also find you get an even better deal, like we did on our mobile phones.

If you can't switch something now (because it is an insurance product with an expiry date), then diarise in your calendar when to investigate the switch (usually 2 weeks before). Also write it down in your *RETIRE NOW! Action Plan*.

Write down all of your savings per month below:

_____

_____

_____

_____

_____

_____

_____

_____

_____

_____

_____

_____

Expense Optimisation

_____
_____
_____
_____
_____
_____
_____
_____

Total saved per month:
£_____

Visit the *My Castle Property community* Facebook group:
- Post how much you have just saved per month using RETIRE NOW!
- Comment on at least one person's post to welcome newcomers and congratulate others on their achievements. Share the love, and they will support you back.
- Tell the world!!!

How to save over 1% of your expenses

How many of those expenses could you switch to a credit card instead of direct debit, cheque or debit card?

Cashback credit cards pay you a percentage of cash each year on your purchases. You must pay 100% of the outstanding balance every single month. The interest rates are some of the highest in the industry (typically 35% or more) …meaning that your debts will snowball if you don't pay them off. You can set up your account to automatically direct debit the full balance each month.

I used to work for a credit card company. The minimum payments are designed to try to keep you in debt forever.

The top cashback credit card is the *American Express Platinum Cashback Credit Card*. It provides 1% cashback up to £10,000, then rises to 1.25% thereafter.

American Express has provided the highest paying cashback card in this market for decades—however it tends not to be accepted in some of the smaller shops, so I always have another card with an alternative provider…

For the highest paying cashback Visa/Mastercard credit card, check Martin Lewis' monesavingexpert.com. These only pay about 0.5% and often drop the rate after a year—so you may find you need to change card again at some point.

Cashback Credit Card.

Exercise 11: Cashback

>   Apply for a cashback credit card (but, only if you always pay off your balances in full each month, without fail).

You can also enrol on Quidco.com to receive cashback on purchases with certain companies. Their members make an average of £300 per year. For example, you could receive cashback on office stationery, train tickets, mobile phone contracts and landlord's insurance. Simply enrol for free, then make sure you click through from the Quidco site when you make a purchase.

Can you Retire Now?

How did you find the previous exercise? It's amazing how much money you can save per year, in only a few hours work.

Exercise 12: Can you retire now?
Deduct your monthly expense savings from your average expenditure per month.

After expense optimisation I now only spend £_____ per month

This is now your real Level 1: Financial Independence figure. Put a neat line through your original figure in Chapter 2 and write this revised figure.

Passive Income per month:
Write down any benefits you are entitled to per month (remember these are only temporary), property income, annuities, and any other passive income you <u>currently</u> receive <u>without working</u>.

I'm going to be tough on you—if you already receive income from property, but are managing it yourself (and don't have a staff member 100%

managing it), then do not include that below—the simple test is…could you go away for one month with no phone, internet or email access and have a thriving business when you come back? We did nothing for the first six months of our retirement. Could you do that? If not, then you have created a JOB. We will cover what to do about it in the Retirement Systemisation section.

	Per month
Benefits (temporary):	£_____
Property income (passive):	£_____
Annuity income:	£_____
Pension:	£_____
Savings interest:	£_____
Other non-working income:	£_____

Total Passive income per month (Cashflow): £_____

Passive income – Personal Expenditure
= £_____ passive profit per month

If your current figure is positive, then you are Financially Independent and could RETIRE NOW!

If you've now realised you are Financially Independent, then write a celebratory post on our Facebook group, *My Castle Property community*. Share your success. Show people it is possible for them to do it too—they will feel inspired by you.

How close are you to becoming Financially Independent? Could you further optimise your expenses to get closer? Could you move to a cheaper area or property to cut your rent? Could you take in lodgers? Could you move into a house share (HMO).

If you're not Financially Independent, then don't spend the savings you've achieved from expense optimisation. Put them away in a savings account and use them to invest in Income Producing Assets (which we will cover later).

If you have trouble saving, then open a separate account that you do not touch and transfer a fixed amount each month. Start with an easy amount, and then increase it by 10% every three months. Always save before you spend.

I remember the day we optimised our expenses and saved £1,000 per month.

I put together a complex spreadsheet with our key property information including cash flow, our expenses, net worth, and passive income. We put in the new average monthly expensive figure. We were Financially Independent, and we didn't know it! We couldn't believe it…Sarah was only 39 years old.

"Why are we still working?" I asked. "And why do we live in a really expensive area in Surrey, when we don't need to be in a particular location for a job?" We realised we could move to a cheaper area like Kent, without compromising on a nice area to live in.

How many years earlier could we have retired? If only we'd done this exercise sooner. With our current property knowledge, we could have retired in our twenties.

What is your Net Worth?

We developed our own spreadsheet to calculate this automatically each month—I recommend you do the same.

Exercise 13: Calculate your Net Worth.

> Assets
> Write down the value of properties, savings, stocks and shares, etc. Don't include cars or personal possessions.
>
> Property: £_____
> Savings: £_____
> Stocks and Shares: £_____
> Other: £_____
> **Total Assets:**   £_____
>
> Liabilities
> Mortgages: £_____
> Loans: £_____
> **Total Liabilities:** £_____

One of the things I've noticed, is that the people who have tens or hundreds of millions of property dress in whatever they want. They are often in jeans, T-shirts and trainers, as it's more comfortable. So, now I don't feel bad about being myself.

I've reduced my obsession with luxury brands. Occasionally I slightly weaken at cars, but I am self-aware and know that prestige should only be a small reason for choosing a specific car—it must still offer something that the other models don't.

The main takeaway for me is that you can be happy NOW. You can have goals, and should have—**but be happy with where you are now.** Having a less lavish lifestyle can mean that you can retire far earlier than if you buy a mansion and fleet of cars…just to impress others on social media.

We now value <u>time</u> over material goods—raising our children, spending time learning, serving people and building our legacy for future generations.

CHAPTER FIVE
Thoughts & Dreams

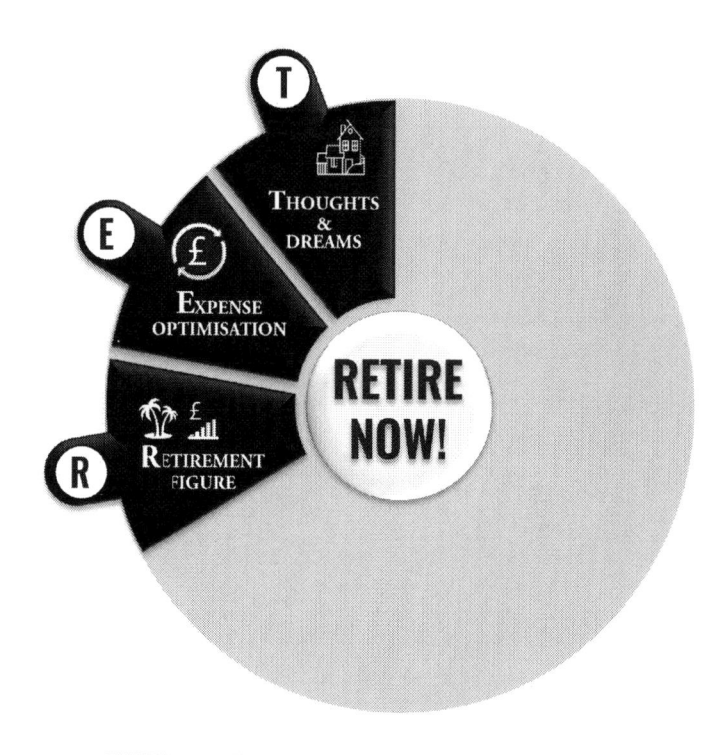

"Chose a job you love, and you will never have to work a day in your life"

—Confucius

What are Values?

Your values unconsciously guide your decision-making. These things are completely unique to you and change over time. You don't realise you are doing it.

You know those awful tasks that you continually put off doing? The reason you delay them is because deep down they don't align with your values.

For example, let's say you don't like doing your work expenses or bookkeeping—you will probably have a pile of receipts in an envelope or your in-tray that keep building up and you reluctantly get around to processing them once a month, or less.

However, you are quick to do things that DO align with your values. These are probably not on your "to do list" as you find yourself looking forward to doing them.

By aligning your goals with your values, you will be able to accelerate your achievements. For example, years ago I went on a course for one strategy that I felt I would create a money-making machine—I wasn't that keen on going on that course, but I went anyway and spent thousands.

Do you think I implemented anything? No. I kept giving myself excuse, after excuse, after excuse as to why I couldn't do it. It was a complete waste of my time and money—I didn't have the self-awareness to understand that it didn't align with my values.

Therefore, it's really important to understand what your values are, so you don't start heading in the wrong direction…and sabotage yourself.

On the positive side—once you know what your true values are, you can dive in headfirst on those to make a success of your life. You will make things happen with less effort.

The values that society put onto you, or others impose on you, are their values—not yours. You can recognise other people's values when you say something like "I really should do that…I need to do that…I ought to do that…I have to do that…I try to do…"
However, when something aligns with your true values, you will say **"I love to do this…I dream of doing this…"**

For Sarah and I, our top three values are Financial Freedom and leisure time; relationship and family; health and fitness.

> "People will naturally act in accordance with their own true highest values – spending money on what they truly value, spending time in ways that reflect what is most important to them"
>
> —Dr John Demartini

Your voids

According to Dr John Demartini, some "Values come from voids." Our values can be created from what was lacking in our lives.

These voids may be from challenges, sorrows, or really traumatic events. One of our top three values is health and fitness. When I was a child, I was weak and fat—I got bullied at school. So, I started lifting weights, which enabled me to become and look physically stronger, which stopped the bullying. Keeping strong is a permanent part of my lifestyle—I never need to be motivated to exercise, as I don't want to become weak again.

Identify your values

Look in your physical environments. Categorise the items that fill your home or personal belongings at work.

For example, with my value of health and fitness. I tried to keep that part of me hidden when I decided to openly come out as a "property investor," as I thought it wasn't very business-like. I decided only to wear suits instead of t-shirts and tracksuit bottoms and stopped posting photos of me exercising on social media.

However, there was an urge deep down inside me that wouldn't go away. If you take a look at my bookcase at home (or e-books), you will find so many books on health and fitness. At least half my wardrobe is fitness gear. My garden shed is packed full of gym equipment. Social media shows a lot of photos of me exercising. The cupboards in my kitchen are full of very healthy food (and very little unhealthy food).

It would be very obvious to outsiders that health and fitness is one of my highest values. Once I accepted that part of myself, I put my suit to the back of my wardrobe and started wearing jeans, a t-shirt and trainers to property meetups! It felt more congruent, and people know me as the property investor who is also really into health.

But what about you? Perhaps if I look at your desk at work, I will see it littered with photos of your children—are there walls dedicated to them at home? Perhaps your family are one of your highest values?

Exercise 15: Identify your Values
If you had to categorise everything, what would be the top five things you identify?

What's in my physical environment?
1. WATER
2. Books
3. Kids
4.
5.

How do you spend your free time? Do you make time for

things when you are relaxing? For example, I go to the gym three times a week. Sarah loves to cook healthy food. What's in your diary? We have the gym blocked out three times a week, and schedule things around it.

What I like to do when I have free time:
1. _Do stuff outside_
2. _Look after the animals_
3. _Go to the seaside / active stuff_
4. _Breakfast with Al._ _with Pam_
5. ___

What topics do you always talk about with your friends? Whenever we meet with our friends, we always talk about two things:
1. How to get financially free through property.
2. How to improve their health and fitness.

These are subjects we can't stop talking about—they are our highest values.

What I always talk about with my friends:
1. ___
2. ___
3. ___
4. ___
5. ___

What do you spend all your money on? Again, I buy a lot of health and fitness books—and also many property and thinking about selling their home...everything is pushing you towards it.

When a new opportunity comes your way, you will be able to look at your dream board to check whether it fits with your long-term dreams—or if it conflicts with them. If it conflicts, you will find yourself dragging your feet and you should say "no." Alternatively, if it aligns with your dreams, then go ahead and do it.

Sometimes opportunities will come around that both fit and conflict with your dream board. This has happened to us before—it made us simultaneously excited and apprehensive. It's not an easy decision to evaluate. Draw up a pros and cons list and see whether one side significantly outweighs the other.

Exercise 16: Design your own Dream Board
Take a look at the example on the next page, then spend 15 minutes designing your own dream board—if you have a partner, create a joint one. It doesn't need to have the same items as the example—it's totally flexible. Do your own thing. Just try not to have too many material possessions. *Be* and *Do* are much more important to giving your life meaning.

It's your life on just one piece of paper. It's not fixed in stone—you can amend it at any time in the future. Keep adding things or taking items away as your circumstances or desires change. When I was younger, one of the activities on my bucket list was skydiving...but you won't see it on my current Dream Board, as I'm not interested in doing it anymore.

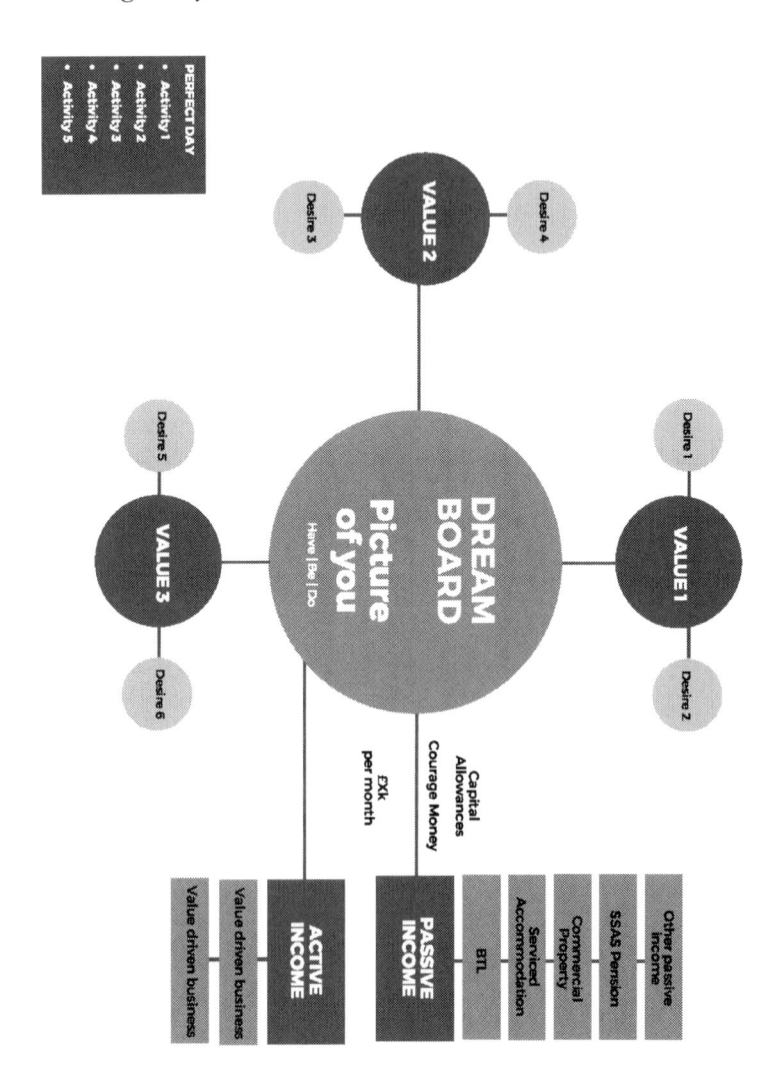

Your Dream Board
Draw yours here.

If you are feeling like sharing, post a photo of it on our Facebook group.

them become bankrupt.

So, the important lesson to learn is that if you had a millionaire's, or billionaire's income—it would not make you wealthy—**you have to know how to keep hold of your money**. You need to change your behaviour and reframe your mind into a wealthy mindset.

What matters is how much <u>passive</u> Cashflow you have and your Net Worth.

We repeatedly sabotaged our financial freedom over the years. It never occurred to us that there was even the possibility that you could retire in your twenties or thirties—we thought we were obliged to work until we were 65, as that is what society told us we had to do.

In our twenties, we spent our money on cruises twice a year. Cruises are some of the most expensive holidays you can take, and we did it for many years…blowing so many potential deposits for houses. We could have added another house to our portfolio every year, instead of cruising.

I also didn't understand depreciating assets—new cars lose thousands the moment you receive the keys.

My first car was a BMW, which I got on PCP. I was only 22 years old. I spent all my money on it and would barely make it through the month without running out of money. It was a really dumb purchase, as I didn't have the income to support it.

Later, I bought a Lotus Elise with cash…and then sold it one year later, losing a lot of money. I bought a new Land Rover Discovery and sold that three years later, losing £22,000. Each of those was a potential deposit on multiple houses.

I could kick myself when I think about how much property I would have now, if it weren't for my obsession to buy cars. We also bought designer clothes and leather goods; I had tailored suits; ate at expensive restaurants. It was all conspicuous consumption—something to show off to work colleagues and neighbours.

Like everyone else in our work circle, we were just keeping up with the Jones'. A funny story about that…we used to live next to the Jones', who are really high earners!

After a while, we made a conscious decision not to try to keep up with others. Leaving corporate life and working from home, also alleviated the social pressure to spend money.

> "Rich people are committed to being rich. Poor people want to be rich."
>
> –T. Harv Eker

Let's face it, when your life is over, what things truly matter? In Bronnie Ware's book *The top five regrets of the dying*, she routinely asked patients about their regrets during the final weeks of their lives. She found five common themes:
1. I wish I'd had the courage to live a life true to myself, not the life others expected of me.
2. I wish I hadn't worked so much.
3. I wish I'd had the courage to express my feelings.
4. I wish I had stayed in touch with my friends.
5. I wish that I had let myself be happier.

As you can see, none of the regrets were about buying cars, handbags or spending on holidays. All of the regrets were about being true to yourself, keeping good relationships and not working so much.

"I focus on Saving my money for Income producing Assets and Wealth Knowledge."

Once you've saved some money, or been given money or a bonus from work, think about how to invest that money into Income producing Assets or Knowledge to increase your wealth, rather than spending it. Once you have invested it to create additional income, then it is okay to spend some of that to go on holiday, to lease a car and so on…just keep it growing.

You should set aside 10-15% of your income for courses or books to increase your property knowledge, business knowledge, mindset, speed-reading, systemisation, personal development or anything that will take you or your property business up another level.

"I take Action, in spite of fear."
There have been many times when we have been fearful about a decision. And sometimes, it leaves you paralysed. So, when those times come…just think, I am going to take action. Just take one step…then take another step.

"There are no failures — only Outcomes"
You will fail. You will fail many times…but that's how you learn. Think about children learning to walk for the first time—they see other people achieving it, so they set themselves a goal to do it. Initially they are unbalanced and unsure of their feet, and they fall down hundreds of times…until one day, they can finally walk.

We have been gazumped by another buyer. We've had to pull out of buying properties due to the damning information in a surveyor's report. We've evicted tenants who were not paying the rent. We've bought properties that gave a poor return on investment. We've decorated badly instead of hiring professionals. We've bought at the peak of house prices, just before they crashed. We all make mistakes. Take advantage of those learnings, so that next time you are faced with a similar issue, you will know how to turn that outcome into a successful one.

"I Focus on Opportunities, not problems. I Expect to succeed."
Poor people see problems everywhere. "I shouldn't go into Buy-to-Let as the housing market might crash…I don't have any money to buy property…I don't have

enough time…"

If all you see is problems…you will never succeed. **The rich and the wealthy focus on opportunities**. And they expect to succeed. They move forward thinking "yes, I'm going to do it! I'm going to make this happen."

You need to do that too. Look for opportunities where everybody else sees problems—become a problem solver.

We have faced overwhelming situations many times—with everything coming at us all at once. What we like to do is to write a to do list in order to get it out of our head—and try to organise it into steps. Sometimes we discover there are hundreds of tasks to do for a particular problem or project—we ask ourselves "What can I do NOW?"

Then we do just one task on the list, no matter how small, and don't think about the other 98 things—just ignore them. Once you've done that step, congratulate yourself for taking action. Then take a rest break and do another small step. Coping with overwhelming situations is just about putting one foot in front of the other.

"Money is Abundant."
The UK's Gross Domestic Product is £2.89 trillion. They are printing money all the time! Money just circulates from one person to the next—it never really disappears There are people everywhere with lots of money. Your family, friends and people you meet have money. Bank

want to lend money. There is money everywhere.

I have really struggled with the concept of money being abundant in the past, and I continually have to remind myself it is true. As long as the numbers for your next deal stack up, then money is abundant.

And there are lots of places where you can find hidden money—we will cover that later. For the moment, just have faith that money is abundant.

"I make Wealthy and Successful people Part of My Network"
In order to take your property journey to the next level, you will get there faster if you hang around with wealthy and successful people. Aim to bring people like that into your network—not in a superficial way on social media, but by having a valuable relationship; even if it means paying them.

> "Focus,
> Believe it,
> Become it."
>
> —SARAH CHOY

Exercise 19:

rite in your 7-day and 30-day action plan
repeat the RETIRE NOW!
·clarations every morning.

CHAPTER SIX
Income Producing Assets

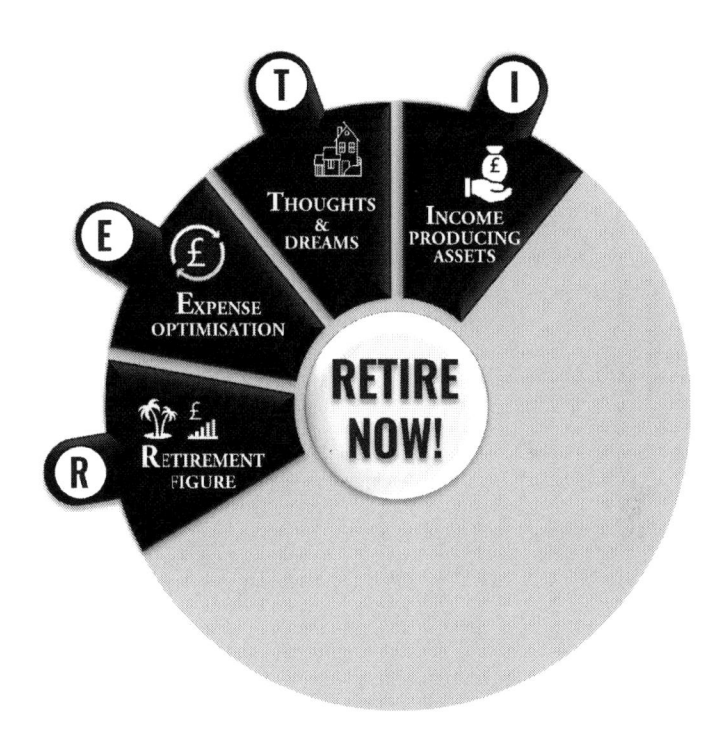

"Ninety percent of all millionaires become so through owning real estate."

–ANDREW CARNEGIE, BILLIONAIRE

RETIRE NOW!

Property is one of THE fastest ways to become financially free. Let us show you why…

Option 1:
Let's say you have £50,000 and you leave it in the bank for 10 years. If you can't imagine yourself having this much money saved, then think about someone else you know.

Let's say inflation is 3% per year. Inflation is simply a measurement of the increased cost of living—these are the price increases on food, clothing, utility bills, transport, household goods and everything you buy.

You find a savings account paying you 1% interest per annum.

With inflation at 3% and your savings earing 1%, that means the real net return on your savings is -2% per year! Let's look at how your cash savings will perform over 10 years.

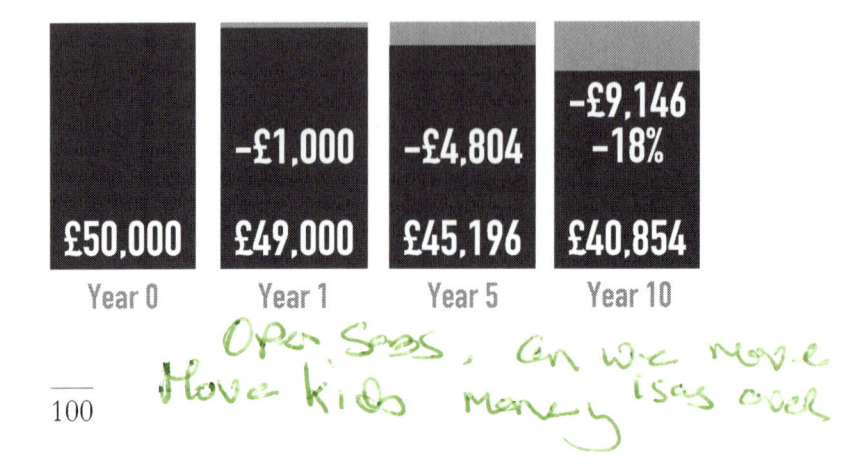

Year 0	Year 1	Year 5	Year 10
£50,000	-£1,000 / £49,000	-£4,804 / £45,196	-£9,146 / -18% / £40,854

Income Producing Assets

By the end of 10 years, in real terms your money is worth £9,146 less than when you started. It has gone down 18%. Shocking isn't it? **This is what happens to people taking the safe option**, every single day.

Okay, but everything isn't doom and gloom…

Option 2:
This time, you use that £50,000 in cash to buy a house. You rent it out for £400 a month, and after deducting your costs, you end up with £300 profit each month. That's £3,600 profit per year.

So over 10 years, you will have earned £36,000. Now I'm sure you'll agree, that's much better than losing £9,146.

But that's not all. Property doubles, on average, every seven to ten years. So that means, the house you bought for £50,000 will be worth £100,000 by the end of 10 years.

Therefore, you made £50,000 equity plus £36,000 rental profit, totalling £86,000. Much better than leaving money in the bank.

I'm sure you'll agree that's pretty good. But it gets even better…

Option 3:
You use the £50,000 as a deposit on a £200,000 house and get a mortgage for the rest. You will be receiving rent

the whole time, which will cover the mortgage and still make you a profit each month.

But what happens to the value of the house? In 10 years' time, that £200,000 house will be worth £400,000! Consequently, if you sold the property, you would make £200,000 profit!

Now you can see the power of leveraging cash in the form of mortgages—you can make exponential increases in wealth over time.

Your home is bad for your wealth

I'm about to give you some shocking news. **Your home is not an income-producing asset—it is a liability**, draining money from you, every, single, month.

Despite what you think, your home is probably not your forever home, as you will likely end up in a warden assisted flat (like my mother), living with your daughter (like Sarah's grandmother), or in a care home.

Home opportunity 1:
However, all is not lost. One option is to turn your house into an income-producing asset like Nicky did.

Nicky lives for free—not only that, but she will eventually own a house for free.

Income Producing Assets

Case Study: Rent A Room
Nicky May

Read the summary or watch the extended interview with Nicky by visiting the RETIRE NOW! bonus resources page at mycastleproperty.co.uk/retirenowbonus

I live in a four-bedroom end-of-terrace house with three floors in Glasgow. Each bedroom has an en-suite shower. I got a really good deal on it and bought it for only £175,000.

My mortgage is just over £600 a month. I set myself a challenge to work out how my house could pay for itself. I did some research on the Internet and discovered that the first £7,500 you earn from renting out a room in your home is tax free!

I'd been rattling around all on my own in this large house and felt I could definitely share it with someone. So, I thought I'd try that and see what happens.

I put an advert on spareroom.co.uk, including some nice pictures of my spare room and the surroundings. Within a couple of weeks, I had a few enquiries. I met with them to make sure I was comfortable with them and weeded out those that weren't a good fit for me. I also asked for references. The best person got the room.

I enjoyed having one room rented out, so I thought to myself "why am I just renting out one room, when I could easily rent out two?"

So, my mortgage is £600 a month, and my utilities, council tax and Wi-Fi come to £280 a month, so I have about £880 per month of costs. I also have a cleaner. I earn on average about £1,000 per month from the rooms, so my lodgers pay for my mortgage and all my costs and I have £100 left each month.

—Nicky

Home opportunity 2:

If you own your home, you could rent out your current house instead. Simply change the mortgage to a Buy-to-Let or Furnished Holiday Let mortgage, and then rent something smaller or become a lodger in someone else's home. Or live with your mother, brother, sister or friend—I've met people that have done that.

Exercise 20: Renting out a rom

Check out spareroom.co.uk to see how much people are charging for rooms in your area:

£_____

Have a look at the "Rent" section on rightmove.co.uk to see how much your home would rent for per month:

£_____

Finding hidden money

Mortgage lenders can provide the bulk of the money to buy an investment property—which could be up to 85% of the funds covered.

You could ask your close friends or family whether any of them could lend you money in return for an attractive fixed rate of interest (not a share of the property)—that's known as "Private Finance."

They are worried that their savings are only earning 1% in the bank, so if you offer 5% or 7% interest, they will earn far more money. That is a really great deal for them and for you. People have lent us money in this way many times.

Or perhaps they could remortgage their house or properties and lend it to you for a higher rate of interest? People have also done that for us. Or you could remortgage your own house, to withdraw some of the equity.

We remortgaged one of our homes to start our property investment business:

> The second home we ever owned was a four bedroomed town house in Kent, which we bought for £164,950. We renovated it and managed to remortgage the house after two years, to withdraw £68,000. We used that as deposits to purchase four Buy-to-Let properties in a cheaper area.
>
> Those BTLs were worth a combined total of nearly £450,000.

Whatever way you manage to raise private funds, you can use a traditional bank lender for the bulk of the finance. Therefore, it is possible to buy property with none of your own money…providing the numbers for the deal stack up—you must ensure there is a good profit margin.

We sold our forever home:

We owned a charming two bedroomed barn in Surrey, which we bought for £320,000. It used to house a tractor on the previous farm. It was over 150 years old, with oak beams and floors, and packed full of character.

We completely renovated it, including all the windows and doors, bathroom and kitchen. We also did a loft conversion to add two bedrooms, making it into a four-bedroom house.

All of our friends lived in that town. Our children went to school there. It had ground floor living, so we knew we could live in it when we got too old to manage stairs. As far as we were concerned, this was our forever home.

However, it was an expensive area to buy houses in and there was a huge amount of money trapped in it. We knew that four bedroomed detached properties provided a very poor return on investment as Buy-to-Lets. It made much more sense to sell the house—rent a similar property in the same area—and use the cash to buy investment property. Then we realised we could squeeze more out of the funds by living in a cheaper area—so we moved to a rental house in Kent, with the added bonus that we would live closer to our parents.

We sold our home for £685,000. By the time we had paid off the mortgage and moving expenses, we were left with £424,000 to invest in property. We estimated we could make at least £1,000 profit per hundred thousand pounds of property investing—so an extra £4,000 a month cashflow…more than enough to move into a rental and live off the income.

Exercise 21: How much equity do you have?
>Have a look at sold house prices (not for sale prices) on Rightmove at your postcode, or within a mile if you can't find any. Select the period as the last 12 months. How much is your home worth?
>
>£_____
>
>How much equity is in your home (value minus outstanding mortgage)?
>
>£_____
>
>Look at properties to rent in your postcode or further out. How much can you rent a similar property for?
>
>£_____

Your pension pot

If you'd like to refresh your memory on why a SIPP or SSAS can be better than an Annuity, then review the pension section in *Chapter Three: Retirement Figure*.

Providing you are not already drawing your pension, most people can transfer their pension pot into a SIPP or a SSAS, which you can use for commercial property investing.

If you have a government pension from your time in teaching, police, fire service, army, NHS, etc., then it might not be possible to transfer it—you should seek advice from an IFA.

You can contribute up to £40,000 of your income into a SIPP or a SSAS, completely tax-free. Consequently, if you are a higher rate taxpayer, then you can reduce your income by doing this. The maximum you can transfer in a single year is £40,000 (providing you earned that much). If you haven't used your allowance from the previous year, then you can add that to the pot as well. So instead of grumbling that you're paying 40% tax, you can get to keep the 40% in your pension instead.

You can contribute up to £1 million into your pension. A SSAS allows up to eleven people, so they can contribute up to £1 million each. You could add your children when they turn 16 years old.

Not only that, but you can withdraw 25% of the pot, completely tax free, when you turn 55 years old. However, once you have done that you will be limited on how much you can transfer back into your pension. Seek the advice of your SIPP/SSAS provider.

A SSAS can also lend up to 50% of the fund to a sponsoring employer (which could be a limited company that you own).

Therefore, you could use your pension to buy commercial

property such as retail shops, takeaways, restaurants, warehouses and industrial units, etc.

Residential flats are not considered commercial property, so a mixed-use property with a commercial unit on the ground floor and a residential flat above it is not permitted be put into a SIPP or SSAS. However, it is possible to title split the two parts, so that the pension buys the leasehold of the commercial part. Seek your pension provider and solicitor's advice before doing that.

Serviced Accommodation is not permitted to go into your pension either. Although it may be commercial in nature, it is too easy to return it back into residential use.

Please be aware that in certain cases, your pension provider might not accept a hotel or B&B—check carefully.

Having a SIPP or a SSAS pension is a great way to build your retirement pot fast—and to be in control of your finances. However, make sure you follow your provider's guidelines on the types of property that can be included in your pension, **otherwise you can be liable for a tax bill of up to 55%.**

The rule of 72

Albert Einstein reportedly stated that compound interest was "the eighth wonder of the world"

The rule of 72 is simple way to calculate how long it will

take for your investment to double. The formula is:

$$\frac{72}{\text{Interest rate}} = \textbf{Number of years to double}$$

For example, an investment with a 10% interest rate will take 7.2 years to double. This assumes that the interest paid continues to be reinvested at the same rate.

This means that your tax-free pension pot can grow at an exponential rate in your SIPP/SSAS.

There's a lot to learn about SIPP and SSAS, so for more information I recommend you read the book:

SSAS Pensions: Creating extraordinary levels of compounding wealth—Mark Stokes
mycastleproperty.co.uk/ssasbook

Many of my property friends have set up a SIPP or a SSAS, and the two companies that they have most commonly used are:
wealthbuilders.co.uk/ssas
xafinity.com

Students can buy a house for free
Do you have a child going to university? If a student has at least two years left at university, they can get a property using a student mortgage that provides 100% of the loan.

The student can then rent out the extra rooms to their

student friends, which should cover the cost of the mortgage and provide income for them to live off—so they can leave university not only debt free, but with some savings, and a free property.

Whilst the income from having a lodger doesn't vary hugely in different parts of the country, the cost of the property does vary. Therefore, if you stick to universities in the north of England or in some parts of Scotland, you will make more profit. Conversely if you bought in London, you would most likely lose money.

The property will need to be secured by a parental guarantee and may require that the parents or grandparents have equity in their home equal to a deposit on the house being purchased.

There are only a small number of lenders at the moment, but you can find them easily on a search for "student mortgages" on the Internet. Each one has different eligibility requirements.

Income streams

You should never depend on a single income stream. The reason for this is that tax laws will change—regulations will change—technology will change the way we do things—political events can impact your business. Businesses that are profitable now, may not be in the future.

Income Producing Assets

For example, there are many HMO landlords that now find themselves in the situation where some of their rooms don't meet the required space standards, or need licensing, so they are selling them to unsuspecting property investors.

When Brexit was first announced, one landlord I know had 150 tenants give notice to leave his properties, as they were foreign citizens.

When section 24 was announced for Buy-to-Let, I heard one landlord mention he would now be liable to pay £250,000 more tax that year. It also bumped many people into the higher tax bracket.

If you only have one form of passive income, then can you weather the storm?

There are many property strategies you can use to balance your portfolio, such as Buy-to-Let, Serviced Accommodation, Commercial Property (across all different sectors, such as retail, warehousing, etc.), Commercial Conversions, Intellectual Property, or create a fully systemised trading company that works without you.

A trading company could be in any industry, not just property—it could be selling widgets on the Internet. One of my wealthiest property friends also has a trading business that is one of the leading suppliers of lint rollers in the world.

Whatever you do, aim to take yourself out of the machine—so that you could go on holiday for a month, or even a year without working in your business.

Courage Pot

We have had some really bad experiences over the years, where unexpected costs have arisen. For example, we had 50% of our Buy-to-Let properties vacant at the same time—we were bleeding money and living on the breadline.

We've learned from that experience. We now have a "Courage Pot" which contains 6 months of business expenses in cash, which we can liquidate within a month or less. This pot is divided into separate savings accounts, that we don't touch.

What this does, is stop you from making desperate decisions. When you have no money and are worried all the time, you come across as desperate to other people— they can sense it, and it turns them off from doing business with you. You will find it a lot harder to come out of the hole.

But once you have this courage pot in place, then when one of your properties has a void (is empty), you don't stress about it—you just accept it as a cost of doing business and know it will happen at some point. Your courage pot will pay the bill if you don't have any other savings at that time—although we try not to use our courage pot.

Consequently, when we buy a property, we not only calculate how much money we need to purchase, such as stamp duty—but we also add on the extra money to be put into our courage pot. This ensures you will always be able to pay the mortgages, utility bills and any other costs for being vacant. We make sure we have the courage pot saved before we go ahead.

So, if you decide to lend money to someone for a property deal, make sure you prioritise having your courage pot in place for any existing properties that you have.

How to hold your Assets—Company structures

> *"Our favourite holding period is forever."*
>
> —WARREN BUFFETT

The benefits of setting up a Company
A limited company protects your assets. If something should go wrong with your company, then your exposure is limited to only the funds you invested in the company—it's ring-fenced, to keep you safe.

If you are VAT registered, then you can claim back the VAT on your purchases.

You can also contribute towards your pension, tax-free.

As a member/shareholder of a company, rather than being a typical employee, you will pay less tax and national insurance. So you can get into the situation where you could earn less gross income than your high earning neighbour who is employed…but you have more disposable income, because you pay less tax though owning a company—for example every shareholder in a Ltd company can receive £2,000 in dividends completely tax free in 2019/20.

In addition, many expenses that you are probably paying for out of your own pocket, can be tax deductible. For example, your trips to visit properties and meetings with estate agents and other professionals are tax-deductible expenses. Hotel stays, parking and meals for overnight stays are also deductible. Are you paying for property related subscriptions or memberships? What about advanced training courses, or Mentoring? These are also deductible. You can also expense business mobile phones, leased computers, and even your company car (in an LLP).

If you own a car in your personal name, then you can currently expense business miles at 45p per mile for the first 10,000 miles, and then 25p per mile thereafter.

There are two main types of company—Limited company (Ltd) and a Limited Liability Partnership (LLP).

Limited company (Ltd)
This is a good company structure for a trading business, a property management company, and also to hold Buy-to-Let and HMO properties.

<u>2019/20 Tax Allowances (excluding Scotland)</u>
Corporation tax   19%
Tax free salary for Directors   £12,500
Shareholder dividends   First £2,000 tax-free
 - Dividends above that   7.5%-38.1% tax
There is also National Insurance to pay.

Limited Liability Partnership (LLP)
These are useful to hold any properties where Capital Allowances can be used to reduce the amount of personal tax you pay. For example, Commercial Investment Property and Commercial to Residential Conversions.

An LLP is also the best way to have a car. If you obtained a company car via a Ltd company instead, then **the tax will be excruciating** as it would be seen as a benefit in kind.

However, each Member of an LLP is entitled to one company car—and you'll be able to expense all the maintenance costs to your company as well—that's quite a saving in tax you would have paid. Being VAT registered will enable you to reclaim further costs. It makes the most sense to lease the car, and to minimise the first "initial rental" payment to the value of only 1 month (so you don't tie up lots of cash). Seek your Accountants advice on what you can claim.

Please be aware that if you have less than two years LLP accounts, then most car leasing companies will decline you…so you may have to wait if your company is new.

Premium models are from £450 - £1,900 a month, but you shouldn't even be considering such a dumb increase in your cost of living, unless you are already Financially Free—otherwise that's another £450+ per month that you need to generate in passive income before you can retire. Learn from my car mistakes—go cheaper, until you've made it.

It is a good idea to have a few models in mind and save your searches for email alerts. Occasionally the car dealers make an incredible offer. For example, at the time of publishing you could lease a £40,000 BMW 4 Series Gran Diesel Coupe for 36 months at only £259 a month— that's the same as a large car for a mainstream brand, such as a Hyundai Tucson, that is worth only about half the value of the BMW.

At the more sensible end of the spectrum, you could lease a £13,000 Fiat 500 Hatchback for only £99 a month.

Car leasing deals change all the time. Some leasing companies you can check out are:

leasing.com
leasingoptions.co.uk
nationwidevehiclecontracts.co.uk

2019/20 LLP Tax Allowances (excluding Scotland)
You will be taxed at your personal rate of income tax:

Tax Rate (Band)	Taxable Income	Tax Rate
Personal allowance	Up to £11,850	0%
Basic rate	£11,851 - £46,350	20%
Higher rate	£46,351 - £150,000	40%
Additional rate Over	£150,000	45%

As an LLP, you will only pay Class 2 and 4 National Insurance, which is more favourable than being an employee. For example, if you earned £100,000 income as an employee then you could save about £1,000 due to getting paid via your LLP instead. Additionally, you get to deduct a number of legitimate expenses pre-tax, which leaves you with more cash at the end of the month.

Capital Allowances—Tax-Free Income

If you have generated Capital Allowances (CA) from purchasing, renovating or converting a Commercial Property then you can use those allowances to reduce the amount of tax you pay. If the properties were purchased in your personal name or via an LLP, then the CAs can be utilised against your personal income this year (and additionally last year if you didn't use any CAs). Thus, if you are currently employed, then you can use sideways relief against the tax you paid as an employee.

For example, if you are entitled to £100,000 of CAs, then that means you can earn up to £100,000 income and not need to pay any tax on it. So, if you earned £100,000 income last year and have not used your CAs yet, then you could reclaim all the tax you paid and receive an immediate refund. How awesome is that!

Most people get confused about the CA amount versus the tax reclaimed. Assuming you are a higher-rate taxpayer…and to keep the maths really simple, let's make it a flat rate of 40% tax—so you paid £40,000 in tax on the £100,000 income you earned from your job last year. If the amount of CAs you claimed was £100k, then you would receive a £40,000 refund.

The CA amount varies according to the type of property and refurbishments—you could receive between 10-40% in CAs on the purchase price, and up to 150% on the refurbishment if "green" improvements are made (in the form of Enhanced Capital Allowances—ECA). There are strict criteria on what is eligible for ECAs, so check that before installing them. Seek out a CA Surveyor, who can advise you on the anticipated CA amount on your purchase—they will need to conduct a CA survey of the property to finalise these figures.

Between 2019-2021 a person can utilise up to £1 million of CAs a year. CAs can only be claimed one time on the purchase of a property, so if they've already been claimed

then you may not receive any. Also discuss CAs with your Accountant and Commercial Solicitor when you are going through the purchasing process, so that the correct paperwork is raised.
If you are buying Commercial Property every year, then it is entirely possible that you will never pay tax again in your lifetime.

One of my friends has over £3 million in CAs, so he won't need to pay any tax on the next £3 million he earns.

However, we still need to pay National Insurance, but this is quite small by comparison, as it is only 2% for income above £50,000. Imagine that—only paying 2% tax!

You can also claim Capital Allowances on a Serviced Accommodation property that you own. You must have had it available for 210 days, and actually rented out on a commercial basis for at least 105 days in order to qualify. So, if you have a Buy-to-Let, it can give you an extra incentive to switch property strategy. We'll be covering both of those strategies shortly.

How to set up a company

Here's the link to register your company on the gov.uk website:

gov.uk/limited-company-formation/register-your-company

It only costs £13 to set up a company. You can set up

your company once you've had an offer agreed to buy a property, as it only takes two weeks or so to register.

It is usually good practice to set the year-end accounting date to 31 March, to avoid paying double tax in the first two years! However, speak to your Accountant, as they might prefer a different date.
Seek advice from your Accountant before setting up your company structures…but do remember to ask the right questions.

Most Accountants will push you towards putting your Commercial Property into a Ltd company. When they do that, ask them why their Accountancy practice is an LLP?

Tell them you want to claim CAs against your personal tax—if they've never claimed CAs before, then perhaps find another Accountant with more property specific experience. Also let them know you want to lease a company car (you would get hit with a huge tax bill in a Ltd structure). After that, they should come around to the idea of an LLP.

Buy-to-Let (BTL)

Sarah has 3½ years' experience at Estate and Lettings Agents—helping people and landlords to buy, sell and rent property. So, she knows the Estate Agent's secrets.

In addition, she personally managed our BTL portfolio, until we decided to outsource it in order to become more hands-off.

Why BTL?

It is the easiest strategy for someone starting out in property. It's the simplest to understand and **there's less chance of making a mistake.** There's a huge amount of housing stock, and plenty of Letting Agents to manage them. There are a large number of mortgage providers with low interest rates, and they don't depend so much on personal income.

We became Financially Free and retired using the BTL strategy. However, we made a lot of mistakes. We bought in the southeast, which has one of the lowest returns in the country—we could have retired faster by investing in the north. But as I like to say, "Property mistakes are like a bad haircut…they grow out in the end."

The only problem with BTL is that the returns are not that high compared to other strategies— so you need to buy more BTLs to achieve the same amount of income as a Serviced Accommodation unit, or a Commercial

Property—however, don't let that put you off, as it's also less risky.

If you don't have any investment property at all, then I strongly recommend you start with at least one BTL property **before** trying any of the other property strategies. This experience shows credibility when doing more advanced strategies such as Commercial Property.

When is the best time to buy?

Average UK house prices over the last 50 years[1]

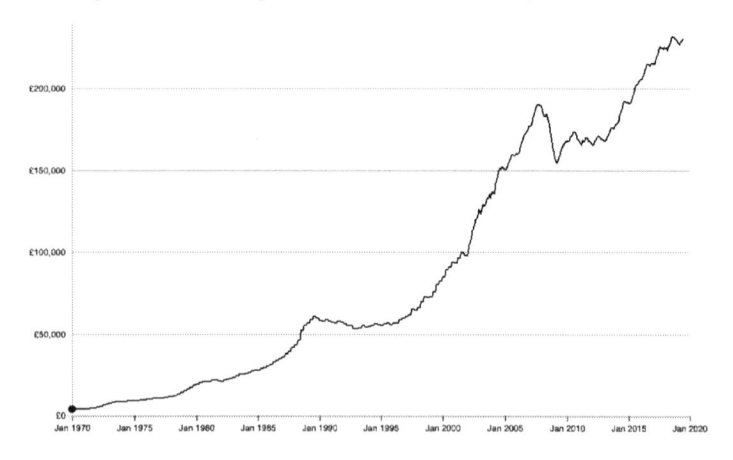

Looking at the last fifty years, you can see two small blips where the housing market crashed, and property values dropped by up to 20%.

---

[1] Source: UK House Price Index, landregistry.data.gov.uk

Contains public sector information licensed under the Open Government Licence v3.0.

However, you can also see that house prices are continually on an escalating upward trend. The very simple reason for this is that there are less houses than the number of people wanting one. This is due to population expansion, and families splitting up and requiring more than one property. The UK is an island with only a limited amount of land, so prices will continue to rise over time.

So, no matter when you buy a property—providing you are aiming to keep it for the long-term, then you shouldn't wait to buy property…instead buy property and wait!

BTL costs
The rough buying costs are:
- 25% cash deposit
- 2019 Stamp Duty Land Tax (SDLT)
  0% up to £150k
  2% from £125,001 - £250,000
  5% from £250,001 - £925,000
  10% from £925,001 - £1,500,000
  Note as a BTL is a second home you will have to pay an additional 3% SDLT (although it is 0% if the property value is less than £40k).
  If you search on the internet for **"stamp duty calculator .gov"** it will calculate it for you.

- Legals could be around £1,500—ask for an estimate.
- There may also be some upfront broker fees of up to £900 to arrange your BTL mortgage.

- Buildings and Landlord Liability insurance of around £150.
- Annual Landlord Gas Safety Certificate—around £60
- Add the cost of your mortgage for the next 6 months to put in your "Courage Pot." At the time of first publishing, the *interest only* rates were around 3% of the loan per annum.

BTL Profit per month

Maintenance and voids	15% of Rent
Lettings Agent full management	10% of Rent
Mortgage[2]	3% of loan/12

The loan amount is usually 85% of the purchase price.

This is only a rough guide—make sure you calculate the real costs, once you have the figures from suppliers.

Getting a BTL Mortgage

Unlike getting a mortgage for your primary residence, BTL mortgages don't rely so heavily on your personal income—particularly if you are buying in an Ltd company. What it does rely on is the market rent expected from the BTL property.

The banks use a stress test, where the rent must be 125% to 145% of the monthly mortgage payments. The maximum Loan-To-Value (LTV) is 85%. Be warned, if you have a BTL in the south of England then you won't

---

[2] If BTL mortgage rates rise above 3% then increase this figure

Income Producing Assets

be able to achieve such a high LTV, as the returns are lower—you might only receive 50% and have to leave in a lot more cash—yet another reason to invest in the north. However, be aware that it is difficult to get a mortgage for less than £30,000.

You can get an idea of mortgage rates from moneysupermarket.com however I'd recommend using a good mortgage broker instead.

There are plenty of BTL mortgage calculators on the Internet, to give you an idea of how much loan you could get.

What type of BTL property to buy?
A good choice is a freehold **2-3 bed terrace house**. Try to avoid leasehold properties such as flats, as there are additional costs to pay each year; and if you decide to use the property as a Serviced Accommodation unit in the future, then many freeholders will prohibit you from doing so.

Terraced properties are much cheaper than semi-detached or detached houses, and tend to increase in value faster than apartments. **Ex-local authority houses are cheaper** to buy and provide even higher returns on your investment.

Remember that **you are not going to live in this property**. If you are a high earner, then imagine the type of house someone earning £12,000 - £25,000 a year would be happy to live in.

The highest yields (returns) and the lowest house prices are in the north of England and parts of Scotland. It doesn't matter if you don't live nearby, as there are plenty of agents to manage it for you.

One inside tip from Sarah…Estate Agents generally undervalue the cost of works in their valuations—this isn't necessarily on purpose, but is because they are not builders, so they have no idea of the real cost. This means that you run the **risk of overpaying on a house that requires completely gutting.**

You should aim for an EPC rating of A-D. This is because you can't rent out a property as a BTL unless it is at least E rated, and that there are proposals to raise the minimum to D in the future.

How to hold the BTL

You should get an *interest only* mortgage (not *repayment*), as capital repayments are not deductible in your expenses. Most BTL mortgages are interest only for that reason.

It is advisable to hold the property in a Ltd company—not only to limit your liability in case you are sued; but mainly to avoid Section 24 "anti-landlord tax."

Not all landlords are aware of Section 24. The implications are that if you hold property in your personal name (not a Ltd), then you can't deduct all of the mortgage interest as an expense any longer. This has resulted in many BTL landlords being pushed into a higher income tax bracket. You can end up making a cashflow loss, even though in your tax return it appears as though you have made a profit.

In 2019/20 you could only expense 25% of the mortgage interest. From 2020/21 onwards, a 40% taxpayer will not be able to expense any of the mortgage interest.

As a simplistic example, if we ignore running costs, then if you paid £4,000 on your BTL mortgage over the year, and your total rent was £9,000 then your real profit was £5,000. Tax on that at 40% would be £2,000.

However, if Section 24 applies to you, then your profit is declared as £9,000 and you now pay £3,600 in tax. This has made many BTL landlords loss-making. Some large portfolio landlords are now liable for hundreds of thousands of pounds in additional tax due to this.

Which BTL location to buy in?

Generally, the north of England and parts of Scotland offer the highest returns on your investment.

At the time of print, some of the low-cost, high yielding areas are Cleveland, Bradford, Sunderland, Doncaster, Rotherham. The best cash-flowing areas will change over time, so don't rely on this list. You must do your own due diligence.

The introduction of the HS1 and HS2 has increased house prices—so areas that used to be cheap to buy houses in, are no longer low-cost and result in a poorer yield.

When cities experience huge increases in property prices, then the nearest town usually provides better returns—so always consider looking 1-2 miles outside.

The property should always be within 15 minutes of the town centre—that is by either walking or using transport such as a bus or a tram.

BTL 5 step process
1. Location
2. Research
3. Power Team
4. Buy
5. Outsource

Step 1 of 5: Location
Pick the town or postcode area you are interested in for your "patch."

If you want to get a very general idea of the profitability of one town versus another, then go to zoopla.co.uk and click on House Prices > UK Area Stats > type in an area or postcode into the search box.

It will show you tables of average house prices and rental prices, for different sized properties in that area. It doesn't

The reason for those days is that:
- They have their weekly meeting on Monday morning and don't want to be disturbed.
- They have a lot of houses complete on a Friday, and may be stressed out of their minds!
- Saturday is often staffed by inexperienced junior employees.

Discuss with the Agents:
- Which are good and bad areas for letting houses. Highlight them on your map.
- Ask them about typical rental amounts for 2-3 bed terrace houses in those streets.
- What are their fees for full management of your property?
- Check they are a member of ARLA or NALS.
- If you don't have a residential solicitor, then ask them to recommend a really efficient one.

You can also look for reviews of those agents on the Internet. However, don't confuse any Agent reviews for buying/selling houses, with renting houses, as different teams usually manage those.

Walk the streets that the Lettings Manager liked. Get familiar with the area. Remember, you are not going to live here—this house is not for you.

BTL Step 3 of 5: Power Team

Get your Power Team in place, so when you find a property to buy, everything can move quicker. It also shows Estate Agents that you are a serious buyer, not a time waster.

You'll hopefully have chosen your preferred Letting Agent after meeting with them.

Find a good mortgage broker. One of the best for BTL is charcol.co.uk Be cautious about speaking with one of the Estate Agent's mortgage brokers—they will try to push you into that. By all means meet them but compare them with others. Make sure that they offer "all of market".

Once you have four or more BTL properties like us, you are considered a "Portfolio Landlord." What this means in practice is that your mortgage application will require a lot more form filling than a first timer. They will want to know details about all the mortgages you have with other lenders—it seems completely pointless at the time, and you wonder why they need so much detail when you don't want them to remortgage those. We've since been through the process multiple times, and now just consider it the price to pay for being successful. We also keep a copy of the details they require in a spreadsheet, so that it's easy to email to the next lender when we need a remortgage, rather than starting from scratch each time.

Introduce yourself to your chosen residential solicitor. It doesn't need to be a company near where you live. Once months—one of ours took six months to let, and we had to keep funding the cost of the mortgage and utilities whilst it was empty.

We learned the hard way. We bought four properties at the same time when we started our property investing business—and all of them needed works before they could be let out. It was a total nightmare. We were bleeding money for months!

Therefore, aim to do another once you have successfully rented one out. Then do it again, and again, and again.

BTL Step 5 of 5: Outsource

Once you met the Letting Agents and decided which one you felt you could work well with, then outsource the management of the property to them and give them two sets of keys. Keep one set for you—however, you can't just turn up at the property and let yourself in; please liaise with the Letting Agent if you need access.

The Agent will:
- Arrange for potential tenants to view the property.
- Check that the tenant has the right to rent the property and carry out ID and credit checks.
- Supply the tenant with an EPC certificate and the government's "How to rent" checklist.
- Ask the tenant to sign an AST contract and protect the tenant's deposit in a government-backed scheme.

great condition that requires little to no work before you let it out.

It's amazing the difference it can make to a property by just painting, adding new carpets and replacing kitchen cupboard doors— "fluff and buff". The easier you make it for yourself, the faster you will get the property up and running.

Note that during voids (i.e. when you don't have a tenant), you will have to pay for the gas, electricity, water, sewerage and council tax.

In order to be compliant as a BTL, please make sure you have done the following:
- Bought Landlord's Insurance (Buildings + Public liability).
- EPC certificate (must have one rated minimum of E, but I'd recommend at least D).
- Annual Gas Safety check if there is gas.
- Electrical safety check is optional at the moment but is likely to be a requirement in future.
- Fit smoke and carbon monoxide alarms (battery operated is ok at the moment, but if you were rewiring then I'd fit mains operated interlinked alarms).

For at least your first ten properties, **only buy one property at a time**, because there will be setup costs, and the properties could be empty for three or more the lines of "I've run the numbers, and the only way this will work for me is if I buy it for £XXX. Is it still worthwhile for me to view?"

The Agent will usually give you a good idea of whether the Vendor (owner) will accept an offer, and possibly the lowest price they would accept.

If possible, aim to view a couple of properties on the same day. This enables you to make better comparisons.

The important things to look out for are any expensive works—these could make or break the deal:
- Old boilers (can be £2,000 to replace)
- Old fuse box/electrics (£5,000 to rewire)
- Roof needs retiling (££££)
- Windows and door replacements (££££)

The condition on the inside, like painting and decorating are relatively cheap—don't be put off by those.

A cautionary tale—on one of the houses we bought, the Agent didn't have a key to the patio doors, so we couldn't go into the garden. We didn't think much of it at the time. However, once we completed on the house, we discovered that what you couldn't see from the inside was that the patio doors were in really poor condition and needed to be replaced—that mistake cost us £1,500.

I suggest you make your life really easy. If you are not experienced at refurbishments, then find a property in property, so you will need to fund those costs out of your pocket.

Next you should **calculate your Return On Cash (ROC)** for a specific property:

$$\frac{\text{Annual Cashflow}}{\text{Total Money In}} \times 100 = \% \textbf{ Return On Cash}$$

Annual Cashflow = (monthly Rent – monthly Expenses) x 12

Total Money in:
- Deposit (usually 25% of purchase price, assuming a mortgage with an LTV of 75%)
- Stamp Duty (use the .gov calculator). Remember this is an investment property so you will need to pay an extra 3% if the house purchase price is £40,000 or more.
- Legals. Assume £1,500 until you have an estimate from your solicitor.
- Renovation

TOTAL Money in _____

Target your Return On Cash invested to 20% or higher.

If the figures look interesting, but it's not close enough to 20% ROC, then calculate the price you would need to pay in order to reach that figure.

Next, call up the Estate Agent and say something along

Income Producing Assets

you find a good one, stick with them!

Assuming you are going to put your BTL into a Ltd company (so you can negate the impact of Section 24)—find a specialist property Accountant and discuss your requirements with them.

BTL Step 4 of 5: Buy
How to find a below market value property

Visit Rightmove and search for properties in the town you've chosen. In the filter, select "Don't show" new homes, retirement homes, shared ownership. When you see the results, avoid any that say "auction", modern method of auction, shared ownership, or retirement homes. **Sort by the "Oldest Listed"** and look for your favourite areas. The owners of these properties may be more motivated to consider a lower offer to buy the property.

Alternatively, and sometimes better, is to do the same search on Zoopla, except **sort by Most Reduced**.

Why might someone be desperate to sell? Well they might be in financial difficulty; or need to relocate to a different area; or are splitting up with their partner; or it could be a probate sale. Whatever the reason, there are people out there willing to accept below market value offers.

If you live in the south of England where property prices are high—then don't just buy the first house you see in the north. Everything seems cheap to me, as each of my houses in the south would buy two or three in the north; so be cautious.

Once you've found a property that looks interesting, you can next **evaluate whether the price is right.**

The way Estate Agents value a property is to look at sold house prices (not for sale prices) on Rightmove or Zoopla to see what similar properties in that area sold for during the last 12 months—they must be a similar type, number of bedrooms and condition. These are known as "comparables" or "comps."

If you can't find any properties that sold in that specific street, then expand the search by ½ mile, 1 mile, and so on, until you find properties. Don't increase the number of years, as that will have a massive impact on the price.

If you have found a property that you'd like to investigate further, then calculate the rough monthly cashflow:

Look up the rent for similar properties in that street.

Calculate the Monthly Rent minus:
- 10% + VAT of Rent for Lettings Agent to manage the property
- Mortgage at 3% interest per annum for 85% of the for-sale price (don't forget to divide the amount by 12 to get the monthly amount)

Be aware, that it may take three months to let the

Income Producing Assets

- Manage any repairs / improvements to be done.

Warning—if you decide to manage it yourself and don't do some of the above within the correct timing, then you are not able to easily evict a tenant. You can join the Residential Landlords Association which is now merging with another organisation to create the *National Residential Landlords Association (NRLA)*. They have some inexpensive landlord courses, an advice line and a great magazine to keep you up to date with any legislation affecting the BTL market. It may be worthwhile joining anyway, as you will want to be aware of any impending changes in legislation.

We recommend you always outsource. We had two properties only a 5-minute drive from our home. Sarah is a trained Letting Agent, so we know how to manage them. However, we came to realise that unless we handed over management, we would limit the number of properties we could own. Our aim was to retire, not to create another full-time job.

Alternatively, there are some local schemes whereby you can rent your property to a local housing association or council. Many will manage your property for a number of years and provide guaranteed rent. You can search on the council's website for the LHA rates. Sometimes the rent will be higher than the BTL market rent—this is because there is an allowance per person, and you might be able to repurpose a second reception room as a bedroom.

However, you must decide to do this strategy from the start, as most BTL mortgages do not permit LHA tenants, so you'd need a completely different mortgage product—speak with your mortgage broker.

Whatever management method you choose, be aware that you'll need to replace the kitchens and bathrooms on average every ten years—so anticipate this cost and plan it into your diary.

In conclusion, BTL is a great strategy for someone who has never invested in property before. It's easy to buy, difficult to make a mistake, and your probability of success is really high. **It is how we became financially free.**

We recommend everyone buy at least one, as it will put you in a good position when you go for lending on other property strategies. Don't forget to buy the property in a Ltd company, to avoid Section 24 tax implications.

Serviced Accommodation (SA)

What is SA?
This is any accommodation used for short-term stays, for holidaymakers, businessmen, contractors, or anyone that needs to stay for one or more nights (but less than six months). You may know it better as Furnished Holiday Lettings or Self-Catering Accommodation.

Almost anything can be rented out. I've seen tree houses, tents, caravans, boats—it doesn't need to be a traditional house.

Why do SA?
It can provide double the returns of a Buy-to-Let (BTL) property—**however, the risk is also greater**. BTL will work almost anywhere, but an SA property could be unprofitable if you don't choose the right location. An SA unit will also take longer to set up than a BTL.

One major benefit of SA versus BTL, is that you can gain **tax relief in the form of Capital Allowances**—once you have operated it as SA for 210 days, and actually been rented out commercially for 105 days.

Another advantage is that Section 24 does not apply to SA properties. Consequently, if you already own a BTL in your personal name, then you could convert it into an SA unit, and sidestep Section 24.

EPC regulations don't apply to SA properties—great if

you have a tree house. Consequently, if you currently own a property that <u>will fail the minimum EPC rating for a BTL, then it will be ok to use it for SA purposes instead.</u>

The other advantage of having an SA unit is that you can take a holiday in it yourself—so one strategy is to consider locations where you love taking vacations.

You will generally have less tenant issues than a BTL, as they don't have any rights to stay longer than they have booked for, and rent is paid in advance.

Your cleaning crew will also be cleaning the property and checking for issues on every changeover, which might be weekly. So, SA units are usually maintained to a much better standard.

We had a 2-bedroom BTL property in Suffolk. Originally, we bought it as a holiday home, as we loved going on holiday there. We read a book on managing your Airbnb property, and it sounded so complicated at the time, that in the end we decided to use it as a BTL instead and didn't get to stay in it.

Ironically, fast forward a couple of years when we had the knowledge of how to run a Serviced Accommodation unit, and now we've converted it to SA and have been on holiday there. It was fairly painless to convert and not as scary as we had imagined. We don't manage it ourselves, as it is a lot more work to manage than a BTL property. That Suffolk property earned £775 a month as a BTL.

Not long after launching we received a 30-night booking as a SA unit, which gave us rent that month of £2,647—equivalent to over three months' rent as a BTL. There's a huge difference in earnings of an SA property versus a BTL one.

You should avoid buying leasehold flats (unless you buy the whole block), as the leases usually do not permit short stays (less than six months). If you already own a flat and the lease doesn't allow it, you could ask the leaseholder for permission, but it is unlikely they will grant it.

Leases are full of complicated lawyer speak, so you can ask your solicitor to take a look and let you know whether it would be permitted—they might charge from £100-£200.

Case Study:
Serviced Accommodation in Peterborough
Richard Snell

Read the summary below or watch the extended interview with Richard by visiting the RETIRE NOW! bonus resources page at mycastleproperty.co.uk/retirenowbonus

I've got a serviced accommodation that we've been running in Peterborough, in the last couple of months. We were running it as a Buy-To-Let over many years, but with section 24 coming up we want to be shifted over to serviced accommodation.

We found an agent who actually runs it from Ashford in Kent, so even the agent isn't local, but they've got all the people set up on the ground — the cleaners, laundry, etc., to run it.

It's been running well for two months so far. It's been full occupancy—through connections of the of the agent, the income we've been getting is about £3,000 a month and our profit from that is between £1,200 to £1,400 a month. Previously on Buy-To-Let we were getting £700 a month; so we've doubled our profit.

In addition, once you're running for a year, we will be able to claim capital allowances on that—so we've got two benefits there. And we got the property refurbed to a higher standard than it had been before. So, all round, it's been win-win, it's been a great story so far.

Richard

Serviced Accommodation 5 step process
1. Location
2. Research
3. Power Team
4. Buy
5. Outsource

SA Step 1 of 5: Location
Either chose a tourist area like Peak District, Devon, Cornwall, etc., or chose a town with lots of business infrastructures such as airports, hospitals, major train stations, power plants, large retail parks, theatres, new or planned housing developments.

Hospitals can be great, because there will be locums who are citizens of another country and are not eligible to rent a BTL property yet, as they need to be employed for a couple of years. There may also be friends or relatives of patients.

Airlines will have cabin crew and pilots that need somewhere to stay.

Planned housing developments could have lots of contractors needing to stay for years.

A good thing to read is your council's 5-year plan on their website—this will tell you about businesses, infrastructure and developments coming to the area.

Ideally pick a town that has chain hotels—so places where

there are Travelodge or Premier Inn, as they've [spent a lot] of money on research—they know there is demand [in that] area.

Check that the council permits houses to be used as self-catering accommodation in your chosen area.

SA Step 2 of 5: Research

Although you are planning to use the property as an SA unit, do make sure that it will still be financially viable as a BTL—this gives you a backup plan, in case things don't work out. Be aware that SA mortgage companies will usually base their loan on the income from a BTL, which will be lower.

With BTL your best returns will come from buying ex-local authority terrace houses—but with an SA strategy, more expensive houses can be more appealing. For example, if you were booking a holiday, you are more likely to book a detached cottage. Larger properties can also give high returns, such as renting out a manor house by the night.

Most lodging in an area is from hotels, B&Bs, studio and one-bedroom flats. However, there is usually very little supply of properties for four or more guests. Thus, if you **bought a 2-3 bedroom house** that slept four or six people—a quick search on Airbnb might show that there are only a couple in your area.

We received a booking from a team of contractors doing some work at a nearby shopping mall. It's much cheaper in a tourist area, then generally the rate per night is more at the weekend. In a business / contractor area, the rate might be more during the week.

Viability calculations—it is useful to do these calculations in a spreadsheet. Overall, you are working out the worst-case scenario of only half the guest capacity, booking half the month.

One of my property friends owns an SA management company, so they are very experienced at marketing them. He told me that one of his properties was vacant for three months, before the bookings started rolling in. Therefore, **don't be tempted to fudge the numbers** in order to make the property pass the test, otherwise you could be accumulating losses from month to month.

Be aware that rates from one month to another can also change. For example, when there is an event at Doncaster racecourse the room rates increase by 3-4 times the normal rate, so you'd want to exclude those unusual months from your viability analysis.

Basic SA Viability Analysis

1. Assume half the number of guests that your property has capacity for—so if it sleeps four, then find properties that sleep four guests but look at the pricing for two people staying.

2. Compare staying Monday to night versus staying Friday to

night.

3. Compare the next month, and the month after to see if the rates are unusual. If there's a huge increase in rates, then exclude that month and pick the next one.

4. Calculate the average price per night (this will probably end up being the price you charge for your property).

5. Then multiply one night by 15 to get the average income for half a month (this is 50% occupancy).

6. Next multiply the total income by 0.2 to get a quick-and-dirty estimate of your half-month profit for a property that is fully outsourced (40% general profit less 20% management agency fee). Aim to make £300-500 a month profit at this low level of occupancy.

For example:
- Average price per night weekday: £100
- Average price per night weekend: £110
- Overall average price per night: £105
- Monthly income at 50% occupancy: £105 x 15 = £1,575
- Estimated 20% profit: £1,575 * 0.2 = £315 per month

- If the management agencies in your area charge only 15% then you'd achieve 25% profit instead, which would be £394 per month

Then go back onto Airbnb and find the five properties you were comparing and look at the calendars of those that are set for Instant Book (not enquiries). You can actually see how booked they are in their calendar. What you will hopefully see is that they are booked up at least 70% of the time—indicating good demand in that area.

Detailed SA Viability analysis

If you have found a potential property to buy, then calculate the real profitability for half the number of people and half the month just like before. Your estimated monthly costs will be:
1. Costs that are a percentage of income:
    a. 15-20% management fees
    b. 15% **Online Travel Agent (OTA)** booking fees (e.g. Airbnb, Booking.com etc.)
2. Example other monthly costs:
    a. £40 Wi-Fi
    b. TV packages (e.g. Netflix for up to 4 TVs = £11.99/month)
    c. Mortgage
    d. Business rates* (not council tax)
    e. Utilities (£150 for a 2 bedroom, £200 for a 3-bedroom property)
    f. Laundry and cleaning £50 x 5 stays (this assumes 3-night stays for half the month)

*Business rates should cost you zero if this is your only SA unit and the amount is £12,000 or less—you can apply for small business rates relief.

Make sure you investigate real costs for suppliers in your chosen area.

In reality, your actual costs should come down over time, as you get more direct bookings and longer stays. Getting direct bookings means you don't pay 15% booking fees charged by the OTAs. And providing you chose the location well, then you should expect to achieve between 70-85% occupancy rate instead of 50%. If you are achieving more than 85% occupancy overall, then it's time to increase your rates as you are too cheap. In general, you should be targeting to make around £800-1,000 profit each month.

SA Step 3 of 5: Power Team

Find a good Serviced Accommodation Management company that offer a full management service, including marketing—don't go for the cheapest. You could pay anything between 10-20% plus VAT. Read the upcoming *Step 5: Outsource* to understand what questions you should ask.

Residential solicitor—make sure they are efficient. They don't need to be located near the property (or you). My residential solicitor is located 1¼ hours from my current home.

Accountant and Capital Allowances Surveyor—after operating the SA unit for 210 days you can arrange for a Capital Allowances survey to be conducted, to obtain a tax-free allowance. Liaise with your Accountant on the claiming process.

SA Step 4 of 5: Buy

SA Mortgage—you will need to get a specific Holiday Let mortgage, as BTL mortgages do not usually permit short lets. None of the mortgage providers on our 7 BTLs would allow permission to also use the existing mortgage for short lets. There aren't many lenders in the market at the moment, so just search on the Internet.

The mortgage will be stress-tested against typical BTL rent for your property, not your anticipated SA income. This will influence the percentage of Loan to Value (LTV) they will provide you with, up to a maximum of 85% loan.

As the property you are buying is not your primary residence, you'll need to pay an extra 3% Stamp Duty if it costs £40,000 or more.

SA critical checklist
Please make sure you do all of the following:
1. Furnished Holiday Let Insurance (Buildings + Professional Indemnity & Public liability)
2. Annual Gas Safety check
3. Annual electrical safety check
4. Fit smoke and carbon monoxide alarms (battery operated is ok at the moment). They must be tested

monthly and logged in a fire logbook.
5. Arrange an independent Fire Safety Assessment (approximately £120)
6. Don't be tempted to buy second-hand furniture, as all furniture must be fire safe
7. Arrange to pay business rates instead of council tax
8. Safety guidelines may change over time. See Housing health and safety rating system (HHSRS)
9. Obtain a Holiday Let mortgage

How to apply for business rates:
1. Visit the VOA website and fill out a form to apply for business rates
2. If this is your first SA unit, then once you are being charged…go to the local council's website and apply for Small Business Rates relief. If you have SA units in different companies, then you can do this once for a single property in each company and also once for a property held in your own name.

I recommend that you **don't buy more than one SA property at a time**, because you may find that SA doesn't work in that location. It could take you 3-4 months to know for certain. And if you've bought multiple properties in the same area, then you'll be losing money multiple times.

Moreover, every time you add another property of that type, there is more supply in the area and occupancy rates will start going down at some point. So just buy one and make it successful—then consider buying another one in exactly the same street, so it's easy for the cleaning team to walk between the properties.

When fitting out the **furniture and accessories** in your SA property, there are companies that are geared up to deliver packs of furniture and accessories specifically for owners of SA properties and HMOs.

They are a one-stop shop for everything such as toasters, kettles, linen, beds, canvas prints on the wall. They provide entire packs, so you don't even have to think about which brand to buy, or whether items match each other. The delivery teams unpack the furniture, put it in the right place, and take away all the rubbish. They set up the TVs. They do everything. It makes your life so easy and relaxing. Don't be tempted to buy flat pack furniture and install it yourself. Keep your life as easy as possible—then there's less risk of things going wrong.

Two companies that we and most of our property friends use are Fusion Furniture and The Property Stagers.

Also, if you join LNPG you can get a discount off Fusion Furniture.

However, I do have a personal preference to get the crockery and glasses from the nearest large supermarket to the property. The glasses tend to be small and thin, whereas you can get some large thick glasses from Tesco.

Buying white crockery is the best way to go, so that it's easy to buy a replacement when they are accidentally damaged.

A typical two-bedroom house that sleeps four people could cost you between £5,000 to £7,000 to fully furnish—that's a lot of money to have locked in a property if you own multiple properties. Alternatively, you can pay for the furniture up front, and then a leasing company can refund you the full amount and you pay them around £180 a month for the furniture in a 2-bed place. We prefer to lease.

I recommend that you always buy zip and link beds instead of double beds or twin beds. That gives you the flexibility to push them together or separate them…depending on the needs of the people staying there. For example, if you have a group of burly contractors, they might be willing to share a room together…but I can't imagine them sharing a bed together!

Also consider getting a sofa bed instead of a sofa—as long as the communal areas are large enough to cope with that many guests. A comfortable range is one bathroom to a maximum of 3-4 guests. Any more than that and they'll be queuing up!

Make sure there is enough seating for all guests in the lounge and dining room.

Income Producing Assets

Having a dressing table that can easily be used as a desk is useful to have in one or more bedrooms. When we're away I occasionally do a little bit of work in one of the bedrooms, away from our children.

Aim to have three sets of linen per person—this makes the changeover and washing easier. Either buy hotel grade linen or rent it. Don't buy the cheaper regular linen, as it will get destroyed in an industrial washing machine, and you'll keep having to replace it.

Sometimes your cleaning company will offer a laundry service as part of their package with you. You could alternatively rent the linen through a company called Stalbridge, which costs up about £8 a week, per person.

Wi-Fi—you need to get fibre broadband. Many people comment that they would rather die than be without Wi-Fi for a day. Sarah and I will specifically exclude any property we stay in that doesn't have it. Everyone streams video or makes video calls, so ensure you get the fastest Fibre connection, otherwise you will get complaints.

Have a smart TV. We like to offer Netflix as it's a relatively low-cost subscription package, so we buy TVs that already have a Netflix button on the remote control. We also put TVs in all the bedrooms as well—because if you've got a group of contractors, and you've got four or six people in the house, they may not all want to watch the same things. We like to give them that freedom.

Always include a washer dryer, to avoid damp clothes being aired out in the property. I like to include a dishwasher as well.

And it goes without saying that people will expect hair dryers, an iron and ironing board, and some basic cleaning equipment in case of spills, etc.

> For an example Serviced Accommodation Inventory of furniture and furnishings, download your copy at the RETIRE NOW! bonus resources page at mycastleproperty.co.uk/retirenowbonus

SA Step 5 of 5: Outsource
Find a good SA / Furnished Holiday Let management company for your property. There are not many of those, as it is a very specialist area. Don't go to an Estate/Letting Agent, as they are not equipped for this.

You could choose a national company where the marketing and listing of the properties on the OTAs is centralised. Therefore, if you had properties in all areas of the country, the management company could all feed all the bookings into one account, so you only have a single company to deal with.

However, on the negative side, if they don't have managers in the area, then they don't know it as well, and might not spend the time trying to get bookings from local contractors that are working in that area—that could result in your property being empty outside of the holiday season and during the week.

One disadvantage of having a local SA Management company could be that they are a one-man band with no employees. I've called up local management companies in the past, and they've told me they have a team of people working for them…but when I kept pushing and pushing, I'd eventually discover that all the "team" are other suppliers on contracts, such as cleaners, etc.

So, if they got really sick, or suffered a fatality, there would be no one who could pick up the work—imagine not getting paid any more, and complaints increasing every week. So ideally pick someone with at least 1 other person working closely with them, who is involved in the whole business.

Where can you find a good SA Management company? Look for recommendations. Ask your property friends. Post in property Facebook groups. Check out guest reviews of the units they are managing on Airbnb and Booking.com. If the reviews are bad, then they aren't managing them very well.

Questions to ask the SA Management company:
1. Do they have a backup person? Are they involved in everything—can they receive, and answer guest enquires? Can they arrange cleaning and maintenance?

2. How much they charge for full management? Do they charge VAT?

3. How much will the laundry and cleaning costs be?

4. How will they market the property?
   They should be listing the property on multiple OTA websites. The top two are Booking.com and Airbnb. If they aren't listing on both of those, then you will be losing out on a huge number of bookings and should find another company. Probe them first, rather than giving them the answers. Others include holidaylettings.co.uk, expedia, homeaway.com

5. Contractors—if your property is in a really prime tourist destination, then it might not be such an issue to only go after the holiday market.
   However, if that's not the case, then if they don't market to contractors and local businesses, you will be empty a lot of the time. Even in vacation destinations, people tend to come during the school holidays and the weekends, so you could be empty during the week, unless they target contractors.

   If they say they do target contractors, then ask "How?" Typical things they could do are to meet with or phone the local employers in the area; take photos of the white vans at hotels and B&Bs and call them up or leave a flyer on their windscreen.

6. What do they do to encourage direct bookings? The OTAs charge around 15% for each booking, so you will make more profit when people book directly on

your management company's website. Do they offer a discount as an incentive to book direct? If you gave 8% discount, then you'd still be making more money.

7. Which Channel Manager do they use? If they don't know what a channel manager is, then that should be a red flag to you. You shouldn't use them.
Some examples of channel managers are Tokeet, Kigo, Booking Automation and Guesty. There are many out there.

What they do is they coordinate the booking diaries between all of the OTAs like Airbnb and Booking.com to make sure there are no double bookings—so when a guest makes a booking on Airbnb, the dates are automatically blocked out of the diary on Booking.com.

Channel managers automatically send out emails to guests with lockbox codes to get into the property and any useful information; they also send emails to cleaning crews.

The channel manager systemises all the communications in their business. If they are not systemised, then mistakes will happen more frequently, and they will only be able to manage about five properties per employee—versus fifty properties using a channel manager.

Setting up your SA unit

You could spend your time arranging all the furniture and accessories, get a handyman to fix things, get a fire safety assessment, arrange professional photography, etc. However, if you don't want to spend the time…you live too far away from the property…or are too worried about missing a critical step, then many SA management companies can charge you a set-up fee to get your property compliant and ready for guests.

This could cost around £1,000 plus VAT for setting it up, plus costs. Once they've done it, ask for a copy of the Fire Safety Assessment and proof of everything they said they would do—don't just assume it has been done, as YOU are liable if your property doesn't meet the regulations—not them!

Once the work has been completed, go and visit the property to check. In fact, **one of our top tips is to personally stay in the property for at least two nights**, so you can see what it is like to live in it. Ask the cleaners to set it up for guests first, so you can see the experience you are offering.

It's amazing when you actually live in it yourself, you start to notice little things—you think "I wish it had this…I wish it had that…" or "That's really annoying." These may be little things that you don't notice when you look around the property.

For example, on our Suffolk property we hadn't noticed

that there wasn't a lock on the bathroom door—probably not a problem if a family is staying, but not great if you have four contractors. I used the shower and then had nowhere to put my bath towel, so I bought a towel rail. If you can't stay in it, then ask a friend who has a really anal attention to detail to stay in it for at least a weekend for free and give you a snagging list. We've done that for our friends (as I'm detail focused).

Property listing
When deciding on the title of your property, it's a good idea to list the town or area in the name of your house, so when people are searching for specific keywords, they can find it.

For example, if your house is in the Peak District, then include that in the title. Assuming it is a house, then perhaps use the name "House" in the title as well. You could also include part of the name of the road that it is on. For example, if your property was 3 Acorn Street, then perhaps you call it "Acorn House—xyz village, Peak District" Or perhaps it is near something that attracts visitors, such as a park, river, or airport? Maybe "xyz view". Think about what you would type into Google to find a place to stay?

Once they have set up the first listing, ask to see it. This is your opportunity to add your comments before they replicate it onto the other OTA websites. Once that is done, ask for links to all the other listings. I remember when we were only getting bookings from one channel, only to discover later that that the SA management company hadn't yet listed the property on all the other websites they told us they would.

Ask them to arrange for a professional photographer, and to stage it. For example, showing a coffee table with two glasses of wine, and the dining table with fresh fruit, etc. This is more appealing to people looking for somewhere to stay than an empty property. You will pay for this of course, but it is worth it, as you will get more bookings.

The most important photo is the 'hero' picture—it is the largest and will be the thumbnail for your property, so it has to be one that will make people want to click on your listing.

When you click on a property on Airbnb or Booking.com you will be shown 1 hero photo and 4 smaller ones—so pick your top five photos carefully. Don't include any photos that could negatively affect the desirability of your property. For example, looking on Airbnb today, I could see a photo of the back of a sofa, looking out of a window onto a car park with a JCB digger—not very inspiring; bathrooms with the toilet seat up; a photo of an alleyway with dustbins and recycle bins. So, if any of your photos don't look nice, then don't include them in the listing!

In general, you only really need one photo for each main room, so include the bedrooms, lounge, dining room and kitchen. If the building is attractive on the outside, then do include a photo…otherwise don't take one. What counts the most to the guest is what the stay will be like inside, so don't feel guilty about skipping the outside photo.

I'd recommend setting the minimum night's stay to two or more nights. You barely make any money, on one night due to the cleaning and laundry costs (and might even make a loss). Once you've got some reviews you could consider extending the minimum nights to 3-5 days if you wish.

VAT

You can reach the VAT threshold very fast. In the tax year 2019/20, if your turnover reaches £85,000 for a 12-month period, then you'll need to register by the end of the following month. You'll have to charge VAT on your room nights going forward.

* * *

A final note on managing your property. If you're goal is to become financially free, then **don't be tempted to manage SA properties yourself—outsource them**. If you do it yourself, then you've simply created a JOB, exchanging your time for money.

I know many people running SA management companies—they've all told me that at some point their cleaners didn't turn up, or people employed by them are sick or have given their notice. One of my friends had to drive two hours in order to clean a property themselves, as a guest was arriving shortly and his cleaners couldn't make it.

People might call you in the middle of the night, because they've lost their keys. Even if you have multiple employees, the buck still stops with you. If you manage it yourself, then you'll be scrubbing toilets at some point, and you'll be receiving enquiries 24 hours a day…it's tempting to keep answering them all day long.

SA properties are much more work than a BTL, that's why we outsource the full management of Serviced Accommodation to other companies.

Managing the SA property yourself, or hiring an employee

This book is all about outsourcing. But if you want to manage it yourself just to get out of your life-sucking daily job—or you want to hire a property manager as an employee—then I highly recommend the following book which goes into all the systems and setup:

The Serviced Accommodation Success Manual
By Paul Smith
mycastleproperty.co.uk/sasuccess

Tax-free SA income

After the SA unit has been operating for 210 days and has been let out for 105 days, it is now qualified as a

Serviced Accommodation unit or Holiday Let. Now is the time to arrange for a Capital Allowances surveyor to conduct a survey of your property, and produce a report, so that you can earn some tax-free income on that property. Liaise with your property Accountant to claim it. Break open the champagne…happy days!

Rent-to-Rent (R2R)

Before you read about R2R make sure you have read the previous section on Serviced Accommodation, as the analysis, setup, marketing and operations are not covered in this section.

R2R is a way of controlling property and receiving the income from it…without actually owning it.

You rent a property from a landlord at a Buy-To-Let price, but then rent out the rooms by the night, for much higher income. You are the middleman taking the profit in-between.

This strategy is most commonly used for repurposing other landlord's Buy-To-Lets into Houses of Multiple Occupation (HMO) or Serviced Accommodation.

It is one of the best strategies for people who are just starting out in property, who don't have enough money to buy property…or for people who will have difficulty getting a mortgage due to a poor credit rating.

Once people have generated enough income from R2R and have built up a pot of savings, most people tend to switch to buying property instead—Sarah and I fall into the latter category, as we already have a substantial property portfolio. One exception to this case is using R2R properties as a holiday homes for themselves—investors at any stage might consider this.

Case Study:
Rent-to-Rent Serviced Accommodation in Bakewell
Abi Hookway

> You can watch the full interview with Abi on the RETIRE NOW! bonus resources page at mycastleproperty.co.uk/retirenowbonus

I like using Rent-to-Rent to turn properties into Serviced Accommodation.

My property journey started three years ago, when I went on holiday in the Peak District with my family. I saw lots of beautiful properties…and I really wanted to get one as my holiday home, but I didn't have enough money for a deposit, as the properties are quite expensive there.

Income Producing Assets

I needed about £60,000 deposit, plus some more money for stamp duty. I asked my mentor Paul Smith for ideas on what I could do. He told me to look at the Rent-to-Rent strategy—that's basically when you rent a property from a landlord as a company let, and then rent it out to guests on websites like Booking.com and Airbnb, who pay you by the night.

Using that strategy was ideal for me because I could get a property, rent it…and I could use it as my holiday home, and also make some money from it.

I started looking for a property by doing what most people do…I called a letting agent. I told them that I was looking to rent a property for five years and what I was planning to do with it—they told me "no, we don't do that sort of thing."

I decided not to let that rejection stop me, so I walked into the letting agents in Bakewell and only told them I wanted to view properties to rent, not the purpose. I booked in to go and view three properties…and while I was on the second viewing of a really beautiful apartment, the agent told me that people didn't want to rent two of the flats, as they were looking for a bigger family home.

The agent told me that the landlord had experienced some bad tenants in the past. That's when I mentioned that I could be the solution, as I could rent the property for 5 years and guarantee the rent—however, I would want to list them on Booking.com and Airbnb, to fill the gaps when I wasn't there.

Luckily for me they agreed, so I got two beautiful apartments in Baslow, Bakewell, on the grounds of Chatsworth House.

I pay £695 rent to the landlord on each of them. I can charge quite a high nightly rate because Bakewell is a tourist attraction—so I charge between £120-£170 a night. So, they make me about £800-£1,200 profit each per month…so I get great passive income from them.

The only problem is that I love staying there with my children, so I get fewer bookings than I could do by renting it out all the time. But I think life is all about experiences. Property is all about freedom for me—it's not about fancy cars; I want my children to grow up having had an amazing life. That's what my Rent-to-Rent Serviced Accommodation business enables me to do.

Abi

Income Producing Assets

There are also investors like Gordie, who focus almost exclusively on R2R and have a huge number of units.

Case Study:
The "King" of Rent-to-Rent Serviced Accommodation
Gordie Dutfield

You can watch the full interview with Gordie on the RETIRE NOW! bonus resources page at mycastleproperty.co.uk/retirenowbonus

I've only been in property for 2½ years—that's not a long time, but I've become a Rent-to-Rent expert focusing on Serviced Accommodation.

I sourced my first Rent-to-Rent from Gumtree—it was a two-bedroomed flat in an area called Govan. If you live in Glasgow, you'd be thinking, "why on earth did he buy a property there?" as it's not a very affluent area. I just got so excited that I could get a deal that I just took it.

That one property paved the way for the rest of my business. The deal was no money down…so no rent for the first month and no deposit to pay—I never pay those.

The rent was £600 at that time. I paid too much, but I think the landlord saw I was excited.

That property is still going strong. I'm making about £1,900 revenue per month and £800 profit per month.

If we fast-forward 2½ years later, I now have 37 Rent-to-Rents across Scotland…from Inverness, to Glasgow, Dundee, Aberdeen and Edinburgh.

My revenue is around £80-90,000 per month at the moment. People managing properties themselves can expect to make around 40% profit. However, I don't want to be involved in managing properties, so I outsource management to my staff—so my profit margin is lower due to the additional costs, so I make 25-30% profit.

I've got another 12 more in the pipeline…then I'll stop for the summer and get some more properties in the autumn. I want to achieve at least 100 properties…although I said I was going to stop at 25 properties, so who knows!

Gordie

R2R is very scalable. Once you have tested one unit in a particular location, you can add more units very quickly. It can snowball into a massive business. Although you must keep an eye on your occupancy levels, as you'll need to move to a new patch when your occupancy levels in a particular location goes down, because you are saturating the area.

Providing you've analysed the viability of the R2R property correctly, R2R can generate a huge cashflow. And **just a couple of these properties, can make most people financially free.**

Speed—I know a number of people who found a R2R deal **within two hours** of looking. You could have the keys in your hand within a week. And you didn't need to put down any of your own money!

That's much faster than buying a property, which we've found takes an average of three months.

If you found and rented out one R2R per month, you could be financially free within 3-6 months.

Is Rent-to-Rent illegal?

You can do many things illegally, if you don't follow the rules.

For example, is it illegal to watch TV? It depends...
If you have a TV license then it's completely fine to watch it. But if you do it without a TV licence then it is illegal.

So R2R is completely legal, if you follow the rules. Businesses have been doing R2R for hundreds of years. Most hotels are not owned by the company operating them. For example, if you go to a Travelodge, you will be able to find a plaque on the wall (probably near the reception desk) stating that Travelodge operates it—but a completely different company owns the building. So, Travelodge are renting it from the property owner, and then renting out individual rooms by the night.

One thing you must do is to ask the landlord to speak with their existing mortgage lender to ask permission to use it for self-catering accommodation—they must do this otherwise they are breaking the terms of the mortgage, and might need to remortgage to a different product. However, a large number of landlords don't have a mortgage, so you might be lucky on this point.

The landlord should already be paying for the building's insurance. However, you will need to take out indemnity and professional liability insurance.

Additionally, you should follow all the legal requirements listed in the Serviced Accommodation chapter of this book.

When it comes to the contract between you and the landlord, you must not sign an Assured Shorthold Tenancy (AST) agreement in England or a Short Assured Tenancy (SAT) in Scotland—that is only for rentals of six months or more and does not permit subletting.

> Please note this chapter should be read in conjunction with the previous chapter on Serviced Accommodation. Information is not repeated in this section.

A four-step process for Rent-to-Rent:
1. Find a potential R2R
2. View the property
3. Make an Offer
4. Outsource

Step 1: Find a potential Rent-To-Rent
You can either contact landlords directly or build relationships with Lettings Agents.

To contact landlords directly, you can find properties to rent on Gumtree, Openrent and Facebook Marketplace. You can also meet landlords at property networking meetings—they usually offer people the opportunity to stand up and do a quick thirty-second pitch at the front of the room, where you could offer them guaranteed rent with no tenant hassles. If you don't fancy contacting them individually, then you could go hire a VA in the Philippines to scrape their telephone numbers off the Internet, and then send text messages to them on bulk, offering them guaranteed rent.

Alternatively, you could build a relationship with an independent local estate and lettings agent, who has the flexibility to work with you on this unusual rental offering.

They might have some properties that they can't let any more due to a low EPC rating—you could take them off their hands, as EPC ratings don't apply to SA. This needs to be a win for the lettings agent, so consider how you could financially compensate them for supplying you with leads.

Before you start offering R2R in an area, make sure you have analysed the viability of doing it—always know your numbers. You will be renting the property by the month from a landlord, at the BTL market rate, or just below it. This is higher than mortgage payments; so don't just assume that once you've convinced someone to work with you that it will make money. You might lose money!

Analyse the numbers—So go back to the previous section on Serviced Accommodation and use the calculations in the Detailed SA Viability analysis, but this time **replace the mortgage with the maximum amount of rent** you can pay to make it profitable at 50% occupancy. This will be much higher than the mortgage.

Step 2: View the property

When viewing the property, check it is fit for your purpose. Ensure it is in 'mint' condition and doesn't need any refurbishing, so that you can get the property listed quickly. However, if it does need any work, then ask the landlord to do and pay for the works before you take on the property.

Step 3: Make an Offer

If you like the property, then you could tell the landlord that you are looking for a "corporate let"—short-term accommodation for your company, other corporate guests and their family—occasionally you might offer it to travel agent guests from Booking.com. Alternatively, you could say you want to use it as a holiday home…but would like to rent it out on Booking.com when you aren't using it.

Don't mention "Rent-to-Rent" as they will look at you as though you have a third head.

You will guarantee the rent for 3-5 years, so they won't have any voids.

You'll be cleaning it to a hotel standard every time there is a changeover, which means that the property will be kept in much better condition than a BTL tenant would.

You will pay for any future damage to the property, and as you are a company, then the landlord has the reassurance that if you don't pay, then they can evict you immediately—that's much faster than a BTL.

You will be renting the property off the landlord, so this is completely hands-free for them. No more tenant headaches.

Terms to negotiate

1. Price reduction—aim to reduce the monthly rent by 10% off the market rent as your company will

RETIRE NOW!

take care of managing the property. But this is negotiable, so if the numbers work at full BTL market rent, then they still work.

2. Ask for the first month to be rent-free. This will give you time to set up the property and promote it for bookings.

3. Break clause—I'd suggest two months notice from you, so if things aren't going well then you can exit. But only allow the landlord to give you six months notice, otherwise you might need to refund a lot of future bookings that you might have received in advance.

4. Don't pay a deposit. Because you will be guaranteeing the rent and will be paying for all damages, there's no need to put in extra money for a deposit. If you imagine you had ten R2Rs and had to deposit £1,000 per property, then that's £10,000 of money tied up that you can't invest in property.

5. Furniture—if the property is already furnished by the landlord at a good quality and meeting fire standards, then great. Otherwise, lease the furniture as mentioned in the previous chapter.

6. The letting agreement—don't sign an AST or SAT. You could sign a company-let tenancy, but make sure it doesn't exclude children or

subletting; if it does then have those sections removed or add an addendum. Make sure you check and amend the notice period.

Alternatively you could use a commercial lease, which is much better suited for this purpose. There are free templates online, such as lawdepot.co.uk
Make sure you state the use as Serviced Accommodation.

Step 4: Outsource
Once you've done all the legal requirements in the previous SA chapter and set it up for stays, then it's a good idea to send the landlord some of the staged photos, so they can see how wonderful it looks. Also invite them to see it. They will appreciate it and will spread the word to their other landlord friends—before you know it, other landlords will be contacting you to R2R. Many landlords have more than one property, so they might hand all of them over to you over time.

Make sure you hand over the day-to-day operations and marketing of the property to an SA management company as mentioned in the previous chapter.

We aren't experts in Rent-to-Rent as we have enough property and capital not to need to do this strategy. To learn more about R2R I recommend the "Rent 2 Rent Accelerator Programme" by Touchstone Education: mycastleproperty.co.uk/r2rcourse

Commercial Property

A word of warning—I don't advocate that people with zero property investing knowledge start with Commercial Property. If that's you, then I'd advise to get one Buy-to-Let operating successfully before you try Commercial.

I've seen a number of people with no property experience take Commercial courses and then still be confused about what to buy…in the end they wait month after month and buy nothing; never starting their property portfolio. Your first BTL will put you in a great position and build the confidence to start Commercial afterwards.

What is commercial property?

It is simply any property that isn't residential (planning class C3). There are many planning classes. You don't need to memorise them, but it's useful to have a list when you are looking at the details of a commercial property. Here's a quick reference table for you.

Planning use class	Description
A1	Shops, cold food, retail warehouse
A2	Financial and professional (e.g. banks, estate agent)
A3	Restaurants and cafés
A4	Drinking establishments
A5	Hot food takeaways

B1	Other Business including offices (excluding A2. Also includes laboratories and light industry)
B2	General industrial
B8	Storage or distribution (wholesale warehouse, distribution centres)
C1	Hotels, boarding and guest houses
C2	Residential Institutions (e.g. residential schools, nursing homes)
C3	**Residential dwelling house (e.g. houses, flats)**
D1	Non-residential Institutions (e.g. church, clinics, crèches and nurseries, museums and galleries, public halls)
D2	Assembly and Leisure (e.g. cinemas, concert halls, leisure centres, gyms, bingo halls, casinos)
Sui-Generis	Anything that doesn't fall within the main planning use classes (e.g. betting shops, casinos, theatres, petrol stations, garages, car park, nightclubs, laundrettes, taxi businesses, shops selling and/or displaying cars)

The benefits of commercial property versus residential property

Longer leases—commercial tenants usually sign a lease of 5-15 years; whereas a residential Buy-to-Let (BTL) tenant might only sign for 6-12 months.

Commercial tenants have very few rights. You can repossess goods inside their property and evict them very

Income Producing Assets

quickly. Of course, seek the advice of your commercial solicitor should you need to do this, as there are specific processes to follow and can only happen after a certain number of days.

What I really like about commercial property is that it is one of the most hands-free property strategies. It requires very little work at all, so you can manage it yourself.

With a BTL you have to pay for repairs, replace carpets, kitchens, roof tiles, etc. But, subject to the lease wording, a Commercial landlord has very few expenses, as the tenants are usually responsible for the costs of maintaining the building—they even pay for your building's insurance! This means that the rent you receive is almost 100% profit. Versus only 65-75% profit on a BTL property, with the added costs of complete refurbishments every 10 years.

Pension companies only invest in commercial property—they are seen as a much longer-term investment than residential.

BTL has suffered from a number of anti-landlord tax measures and regulations. None of these apply to Commercial.

In addition, when you buy or convert a commercial property, you may be able to claim up to 150% in the form of Capital Allowances, to give you some tax-free income.

When you are buying small houses, sometimes there can be a buying frenzy, so you need to put in an offer quickly. But there isn't so much of a hurry with Commercial, as only a tiny percentage of property investors are buying in this sector.

Unlike residential property, you can put a Commercial property into your SSAS or SIPP pension.

An example Commercial property from our portfolio is a "shop and uppers" in the South East. On the ground floor is a restaurant; a solicitor tenants the first and second floors.

We purchased the property for £320,000. It pays us an income of £32,000 a year, which is £2,667 a month. That's 10% Yield, which we will discuss later. For many people, that one property would make them Financially Free—job done, put up your feet and RETIRE NOW!

Do you have that amount of money as equity in your home? Could you sell your home, move into a rental and buy the above property? It's worth thinking about.

Just by comparison, a similar residential property would only generate rent of £1,200 a month in the same area, and then there would be expenses. This means that the Commercial equivalent is paying us just over two times what a residential property can earn in our area.

The remaining lease was 5 years for the solicitor and 10 years for the restaurant.

We bought it off-market via a commercial surveyor that we have built a relationship with. The tenants were completely unaware the property was being sold until we had purchased it—so there were no agent boards up.

We managed to view the restaurant premises just before the new tenant moved in. However, we weren't able to view the offices, but did see some photos taken by a surveyor, who noted that the rear windows needed repairing. We looked at the outside ourselves and overall it looked ok.

We made it a condition of the sale that the vendor repaired the rear windows before we purchased. They would have recharged the cost to their tenants.

* * *

Here's another great example of "buying income."

Case Study: Commercial Property in Shropshire
Kirsty Darkins and Jamie MacPherson

You can watch the full interview with Kirsty and Jamie on the RETIRE NOW! bonus resources page at mycastleproperty.co.uk/retirenowbonus

Hi I'm Kirsty. I am a commercial surveyor. I found the deal through one of my clients—a parade of shops in the small market town in Shropshire.

They didn't want it any more as it didn't fit their strategy...but I'm quite happy to have it.

It's a nice, simple, straightforward "buying some income" deal. The rent is £43,000 per annum, with a 10% yield on purchase.

There is a bit of room for us to uplift the capital value, in time, but it is mainly an income purchase. The businesses are all convenience and service retail— Vets4Pets, a recruitment consultant, nail bar and barbers.

Case Study: Commercial Property—Takeaway
Fayyaz Rahman, Blu Bridge Properties in Glasgow

You can watch the full interview with Fayyaz on the RETIRE NOW! bonus resources page at mycastleproperty.co.uk/retirenowbonus

I bought a hot food takeaway. It's not a very big shop—just 500 square feet.

I own a laundrette business next to a takeaway, about 12 miles outside Glasgow. A couple owned the Chinese takeaway and they ran it themselves. They worked seven days a week and didn't have a social life. I saw the husband regularly, and one day he was looking a bit depressed—so I asked him if he wanted to sell the shop…he was so relieved that I had asked, as he wanted to sell the shop discretely, off-market.

The owner asked for £55,000, which I felt was a really good price as I have some experience in the hot food trade myself. So, I didn't haggle. We shook hands there and then, and so in five minutes we had agreed the sale. He agreed to leave all the fixtures and fittings there.

To advertise the property, I made a small five-line advert on my computer and I put them in the cash and carry in

Glasgow. The advert was really responsive…I was getting about a dozen phone enquiries a day.

A Chinese girl approached me. She said, "what sort of key money do you want?". I said, "Make me an offer I can't refuse."

She offered me £20,000 key money. I asked her how soon she wanted to take over — she said "today!"

I couldn't arrange things on the same day, so I told her "put your offer in today and we'll see how soon we can sort out the paperwork."

We bought the takeaway in the middle of June and she got the keys on 10th of July, about three weeks later. That's pretty quick.

She paid rent of £800 a month, £9,600 per annum. We'd agreed a long 33-year lease, with rent reviews every 3 years.

A year later the girl offered to buy the building for £150,000, but I said it wasn't for sale at that time, as that's my pension pot.

Fayyaz

A word of warning…buying and owning Commercial property requires learning a whole new language. It has a lot of unusual terms that you may never have heard before, and you need to understand the basics of leases, and a different way of calculating the returns…it is not really advisable for your first investment, unless you have a mentor or coach—don't be afraid to pay someone in order to avoid an expensive mistake.

I'd recommend a low-cost Buy-to-Let in the north of England for your first purchase, as it will provide you with a quick win and will show commercial lenders that you have some property experience.

The 5 step Commercial Property buying process:

1. Location
2. Research
3. Power Team
4. Buy & Legals
5. Manage

SA Step 1 of 5: Location

The great thing about Commercial property is that it provides the same returns in any region of the country. This is very unique to Commercial property.

Therefore a 10% Yield in London is the same return as a 10% Yield in Birmingham, Hull, or anywhere else—this is because the Yield is calculated in exactly the same way.

The country is your oyster. Firstly, decide for yourself how far you're willing to travel from your home, and draw a circle around that area. We try not to go past 40 minutes, as that's nearly an hour-and-a-half round trip of lost time.

Secondly, find towns with good levels of economic activity within your search area—lots of employment, large companies, train station, airport, hospitals, etc.

SA Step 2 of 5: Research

Find local commercial surveyors in your chosen towns; these are usually also commercial agents. So if you look on the "Commercial" tab on Rightmove and search for property for sale in those areas, you'll see properties and the agents that are listed. Go and meet with them. Try to build a relationship.

Commercial surveyors want the easy life—they want to sell properties by doing the least amount of work. Consequently, many of the best property deals don't make it to Rightmove or the other Commercial property portals…just like the restaurant that I bought.

When a landlord puts a property on the market, the agent would much rather just phone someone up from their little black book instead of taking photos, measuring the rooms and uploading a listing to the internet. We didn't see any photos or a description when we were offered the restaurant.

However, you can also look on the internet.
- rightmove.co.uk
- zoopla.co.uk
- propertylink.estatesgazette.com
- eigpropertyauctions.co.uk
- the websites of your local Commercial Surveyors

If a property seems too cheap to be true, it might because they are selling the business or remaining lease, not the actual property—so **check carefully that the price includes the Freehold** of the property (not a lease). The owner of the business is probably planning to close down, so you would have to employ staff, operate and market this business yourself, whilst paying the real landlord rent every month…probably not what you had in mind.
I see so many newbies think they have found a bargain, as they don't fully understand what is being offered for sale.

Two websites that sell businesses with or without property are:
- daltonsbusiness.com
- uk.businessesforsale.com

You can also discover properties for sale by networking at a business or property meeting. I find business meetings are better suited, as you can speak to business owners to find out what is going on in the town, and perhaps if people are looking for a property to rent or planning to sell.

What type of Commercial property to buy?

Retail—the high street is changing. Businesses are being moved online. Most banks, building societies and estate agents are disappearing from the high street, to become more centralised. Amazon is a formidable competitor in the retail sector—so it is important to be amazon and Internet proof. Betting shops have been closing due to changes in the gambling laws. Pubs are in decline as most people drink at home.

Consequently, when it comes to retail, have a think about which businesses you have to physically take your body to, and can't buy online. These are things like coffee shops, restaurants, nail bars, dentists, chiropractors, and even tattoo parlours.

Warehousing and industrial units—there's good demand due to people selling online. The products have to be stored and dispatched from somewhere.

Office space—interestingly office space had been declining but is starting to become more in demand. This is because there was a change in the planning law, making it easier to convert offices into residential properties. This has resulted in a reduction of available office space, so in some towns the rents are going up.

Calculating the Yield

The value of a Commercial property is calculated according to the Yield. This is not the usual ROI calculation used for Buy-to-Let, so people find it

Income Producing Assets

confusing initially.

If it is tenanted, a commercial surveyor will calculate the % Yield according to the *covenant* (strength of the tenant) and the length of the lease. Or they value it for an *alternative use*, which is usually the *bricks and mortar* or *market value* of the property.

If you plan to use bank finance, then they will also have their own commercial surveyor visit the property, to decide whether they agree with the yield and value.

The lower the percentage Yield, the stronger the tenant. For example, a global chain of coffee shops might be assigned a 6-8% Yield.

On the other hand, a tenant with a high Yield such as 15% is considered weaker, as they are more likely to go out of business.

A strong tenant with a low Yield will result in a higher valuation, meaning it will cost more to buy. But it provides less cashflow than the high yielding property. Consequently, you need to balance reliability against cashflow.

For example, a well-known global brand could be 5-8% Yield.

A local established business might be 10%.

RETIRE NOW!

A new start up could be 15% Yield.

Use these Yields as a guide, as to whether a property is on the market at the right price. However, don't just take the agent's word for it…sometimes landlords just want more money (or the agent over-promised), so the property is on the market at a yield lower than it should be for the type of tenant in place…or even no tenant. I've seen so many vacant Commercial properties on Rightmove priced as though a really premium brand is in place—it's crazy.

Okay, onto the formula…

$$\frac{\text{Annual Rent}}{\text{Property Value}} \times 100 = \text{\% Gross Yield}$$

For example:
    A global coffee shop brand
    Annual Rent: £35,000
    Property for sale at: £450,000
    Gross Yield:
    (£35,000 ÷ £450,000) × 100 = 7.8%

Exercise 24: Calculate Commercial Property Gross Yield

Get to the same Gross Yield using the rent and purchase price:
    Example 1:
    Annual Rent: £25,000
    Property for sale at: £250,000
    Gross Yield: *10%*

Example 2:
Annual Rent: £15,000
Property for sale at: £100,000
Gross Yield: *15%*

Sometimes you will see the *Initial Net Yield* in property details—this is usually after deducting purchasing costs such as stamp duty, which can make it difficult to compare. Nonetheless, calculate it yourself using the Gross Yield formula.

For instance, if you see a property with an annual rent of £20,000 and you feel that the type of tenant in place should have a 10% Yield, then it leads to a value of £200,000. Consequently, if the property is for sale at a higher price than your calculation, then you know it is over-priced.

Please be aware that deciding on a Yield is slightly more of an art than a science. You may see well-known brands with different surveyors showing Yields varying up to 2% all over the country.

How to calculate the Value of a Commercial property. Reversing the formula, we can work out how much a property should be worth.

$$\frac{\text{Annual Rent}}{\text{\% Gross Yield}} = \text{£ \textbf{Value}}$$

For example,
Annual Rent: £20,000
Gross Yield: 9%

£200,000 ÷ 0.09= £222,222 Property Value

Other frequently used terms:
Rent PAX—Rent per annum exclusive (does not include running costs such as VAT, business rates, insurance, etc.) So, it's still just the annual rent, but written in a more confusing way.

Mixed use Commercial—it could include two or more different use classes. For example, it is quite common to see a shop with a residential flat above it. If you see one for sale, then value the residential part separately from the Commercial part—it's as simple as visiting three of the local residential estate agents and asking them. Be aware that flats above Commercial property are worth less than dedicated residential blocks of flats as they are more difficult to finance and less desirable.

General lease terms
You will usually see some of the lease highlights written in property details. These details are really important, as it will make or break whether you should go for the deal. If you've checked the numbers and it looks interesting, then request a full copy of the lease.

Income Producing Assets

Term—how long the tenant is renting the property for. This could be for any number of years. However, the average lease length is 7 years. Bank lenders usually require at least 5 years remaining.

Break clause—allows the tenant or landlord to break the lease before the end of the term. Lenders prefer no break for at least the next 3 years. Be cautious if a break is coming up soon.

License to occupy—this is a simpler lease than a fixed term lease. It's often used as short-term stopgap, whilst the landlord looks for a permanent tenant. However, you must treat this with caution, as once the tenant has been there for 6 months, they develop rights and can demand a fixed term lease with the same terms they had from the start. It could be difficult to get them out.

Full Repairing and Insuring lease (FRI)— is where the tenant is liable for all the repair costs. This is the best type to have, as it means you have zero maintenance costs! You can also charge for the building's insurance, as long as it is in the lease.

Virtual FRI—when you have two or more tenants who are responsible for the maintenance of the building between them/proportionately. Check all the leases carefully.

Internal Repairing Insuring Lease—this is when the tenant only pays for maintenance of the inside of their unit. If they have no responsibility for the building/communal area costs, then you will likely have to suck up some of these costs…so it isn't as attractive as an FRI lease.

Rent Reviews—these could be upward only; open market; or RPI.

SA Step 3 of 5: Power Team
You are going to need a slightly different power team from the one you used for a BTL or SA.

Commercial Surveyor/Agent—they can advise you on rent expectations and can help you to find properties to purchase.

Commercial Broker—go to a specialist one that focuses on Commercial mortgages. They will put your case to the most appropriate lenders for your current situation and the property.

Commercial Solicitor—go to one that is dedicated to Commercial. Don't choose a residential one that does a bit of commercial on the side.

Accountant—chose one that understands Commercial property, residential property, and the tax implications such as Capital Allowances. It can be useful to buy the property in an LLP, so that you claim tax-free CAs against your personal income. If you put the property in a Ltd company instead, then you will only receive CAs against the profit of the Ltd company (not your personal income).

Seek your Accountant's advice.

Capital Allowances Surveyor—you should be able to use the same one you used for a Serviced Accommodation CA survey.

SA Step 4 of 5: Buy & Legals

If you need a mortgage, then the property must have an existing tenant in it.

"Can I get a commercial mortgage when I don't have any Commercial property already?"

This is a question I get asked all the time. When we bought our first Commercial property, we set up a new LLP company with no trading history and had a choice of lenders willing to provide a mortgage.

The lender will send a commercial surveyor to conduct a valuation, to make sure it is worth what you think it is worth. The lender will charge you for this. If you have any doubts as to whether you'll be able to get a mortgage on a specific property, speak with your commercial broker.

If the Commercial property is vacant, then you need to buy the property with cash…fill it with a tenant…then you can apply for traditional bank finance. Alternatively, if you can find a potential tenant and get them to sign an *Agreement for Lease* before you exchange, then you can raise bank finance. Be cautious though, as it is not necessarily a quick process to find a tenant, and if you have your numbers wrong then you might end up getting less rent than you thought.

If you are looking for premises for your company and it has been trading for at least 2 years, you can sign an Agreement for Lease to occupy a vacant property and apply for a mortgage before you purchase it. That's almost like printing money. Buy it cheap, then raise the value of the property by having you as a tenant. Look at the previous Yield calculation to estimate how much the property would be worth.

You can also buy Commercial property using a SIPP or SSAS. Check with your provider on the terms and criteria.

SA Step 5 of 5: Manage
Commercial property is relatively easy to manage. You can do it yourself.

You need to send your tenants an invoice once a month or on the "usual quarters" (as specified in the lease). I prefer monthly, with a regular fixed payment. We put ours into the accounting system Xero, so it actually raises the monthly invoice for us. Zero effort!

It's good practice to pop in and see your tenants every couple of months to check the property is well maintained. It is also advisable to meet six months prior to a break clause to see whether they are planning on staying.

If you have any queries going forward, simply ask either your Commercial Surveyor or Solicitor—that's why you need them in your power team.

Don't be a loser

There are many advanced property strategies that you will hear about, such as lease options, commercial to residential conversions, filling commercial properties with brands, and many more. They all sound great…

However, what I've observed when mentoring people is that some will focus on the "unicorn"—that is the one dream deal that will bring them a huge amount of money; so they disregard everything else…when I see these people 12 months later, they have typically achieved NOTHING.

Accordingly, I would like you to **think about your property business as a road trip**, with a number of increasingly more expensive tollbooths along the way. Start with the absolutely easiest property purchase first—your likelihood of succeeding will skyrocket. Don't do anything fancy at all. Once you've achieved a successful result, you'll have learned a lot in the process and have more confidence to try a larger or more complicated deal next time.

What can you expect to achieve?
If you don't have much cash, you should be able to find a Rent-to-Rent property to use as Serviced Accommodation

in less than one day, and have it running within a month. Some of my property friends have found a R2R within two hours or less, and with young children accompanying them.

If you have savings, then you should be able to purchase a low-cost Buy-to-Let in the North of England within an average of three months; or purchase an already tenanted Commercial property within 3-6 months.

Always start with only one unit in a location and wait until it is producing income before buying another.

And rather than sinking all of your money into one property, I prefer to spread my funds across multiple properties, so I can diversify the risks. Because at some point, one of them will be empty—and if that is your only property, then you will go from cash flowing to making a loss every month.

Exercise 25: Which property strategy will you do?
Update your 7, 30 and 90-day action plan with the tasks you plan to do to start or accelerate your property investing portfolio.

CHAPTER SEVEN
Retirement Systemisation

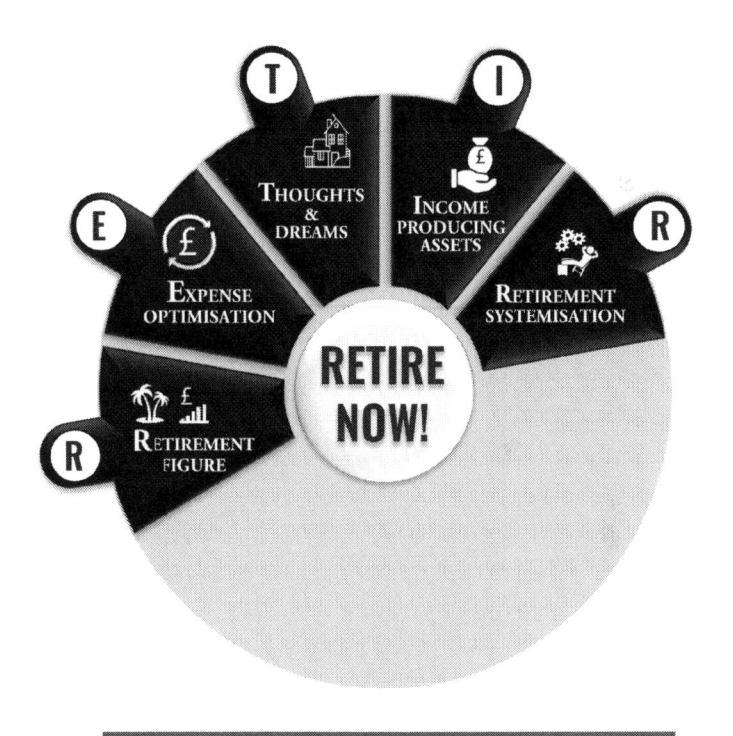

"The rich invest in time, the poor invest in money."

—Warren Buffett

We all get 24 hours a day. It's just that some people are able to squeeze more value out of that time than others.

The "Rich" know that time is their most precious resource. To become truly successful…you need to learn to work on your business, rather than in your business.

We realised a long time ago that managing, cleaning and decorating properties ourselves would slow the growth of our property portfolio. In the past, we've cleaned toilets, cleared out maggots from a fridge, painted walls and tiled bathrooms through the night, showed potential tenants around properties, and so on.

We didn't realise it at the time, but doing these things ultimately reduces how much money you can make, and it becomes difficult to scale your business.

For example, let's assume you are a masseuse who spends one hour per client. The most clients you can take on per day is seven. You are now at 100% capacity and do any more work. Consequently, the only way to earn more is to outsource that job. You hire a team of people instead, and make only slightly less than you did before, for a lot less work. You could earn £6,000 a month and have to work a 40-hour week…or you could earn £5,000 a month and retire. Think about it.

Once you outsource your properties, instead of spending your time doing £10 an hour cleaning jobs, you can spend your time searching for property and analysing deals instead—to earn the bigger rewards.

Sarah and I have a target to try to manage our entire property portfolio in one hour or less per month. And also, to be able manage it virtually from anywhere in the world. So even if we are on vacation, or move to a different part of the UK, our business is still going strong.

Two of the BTLs we bought were only a few minutes from one of our previous homes. Sarah has worked for an Estate and Lettings Agent, so she knows how to manage other people's properties. We realised that all the wealthy investors outsourced their properties. However, because we had the knowledge, it wasn't easy for us to let go and start paying agent fees—but eventually we did it and have not looked back.

However, when you think about all the work the agent has to do to get a tenant, regularly inspect the properties, coordinate repairs, the administration tenants of leaving, staying up-to-date on BTL landlord legislation…that's a lot of work for them to do for only £50 to £100 a month. And sometimes our Agent's have had to do some awful jobs, dealing with difficult tenants and other issues.

Hence if you currently have a day job, then save what you can to raise money for property investing. I don't recommend you leave your job until you have enough income to become Financially Independent (level 1).

If you leave your job before then, it will take you a lot

longer to be in a position to retire. And as our method is to completely outsource everything, then it's no problem to have your day job and own multiple properties at the same time, as it takes you very little effort. Consequently, if I had a full-time job now, I could still squeeze in one hour a month to work on my property portfolio.

Imagine if you only needed to work one hour a month? How would you spend your time? **It's amazing having that freedom to choose how you spend your time.**

Start with the end in mind and outsource everything from the beginning—don't wait years like we did.

Finding more time to spend on property investing

A lot of people give the excuse that they are working, so they don't have time to spend property investing.

When we remortgaged our house to build an investing pot, we spent every weekend visiting towns and talking with letting agents until we had decided on an area.

Once we had chosen the area and had a good understanding of local rents and house prices, it was a matter of only a few weeks before we had agreed to buy four houses.

Read on to increase your productivity and save time…

Exercise 26: How do you spend your time?

Track the number of hours you spend on different

activities, both on one day during the week, and one day at the weekend. Put it in your calendar now, to make sure you do it this week.

Draw a smiley face against things you like doing, and an unhappy face against the things you find difficult or hate doing. Note the things that are taking you a lot of time.

Afterwards have a think about which of those elements you could outsource or automate—then add them to your action plan.

When we initially did this exercise, we discovered that Sarah spent a lot of time on housework…so we hired her mum to clean our house once a week, and her dad to do the gardening.

I disliked washing the car and kept putting it off every week. So now we get it washed whilst we are shopping at the supermarket or picking up our children from school.

Childcare takes up a lot of time, particularly during the school holidays. When the children are on holiday (but we aren't away), we now put them into all day kids' sports clubs a couple of days a week. This gives us adults time to go to the gym and have days out—and they really enjoy the time playing with their school friends. It's also a lot cheaper than sending them to a childminder.

Not all outsourcing has to cost money. Our only

babysitter is Sarah's mother, so we moved closer to her home, which gave us more free childcare than we had previously. There were also some tasks that Sarah hated, but I enjoyed or was indifferent about—so we swapped.

Social Media
Most people spend time on social media. When I tracked how I was spending my time, I found I was spending at least one hour a day on Facebook. All social media can be a real time suck. Once you start looking at those videos of funny cats, hours and hours will pass you by…

Two things that have helped me are:
1. Restrict the number of times I go on Facebook
2. Turn off as many notifications as possible

I try to only go on Facebook twice a day now; or if I'm not losing time by doing it—such as standing in a queue in a shop. It's also good to have a key objective in mind, such as to promote something; or help two people, rather than mindlessly surf.

Notifications—what really annoys me is all the numbers on the notifications bell and any audio or visible alerts on your phone, particularly on the locked screen. These interrupt your train of thought, making it slower to complete tasks. Go into your phone settings menu and turn off the alerts. Because if your phone is sitting next to you and something flashes up on the screen, or dings…you will look at it.

I remember once being put into a WhatsApp group, and hearing a ding every ten seconds, as people replied. I could feel my stress levels rising—it was making me feel anxious. I could have turned off the notifications from that group, but I decided to leave the group instead.

I also recall a time when I was personal training a client, and her husband would text her every minute, whilst she was training. The texts weren't anything important, but it distracted her the whole time. In the end I had to get her to turn her phone off, so we could focus.

At one point I was receiving email notifications from Facebook and YouTube, so I switched that off too.

If you are in any Facebook groups, the default is to notify you of all posts. Go into the settings and switch it off—unfortunately you have to do it individually for each group at the moment.

In fact, **"Social Media Anxiety Disorder" is a real mental health condition.** So, take precautions. Turn off audible alerts and banners—and only check once or twice a day at the most. Be ambivalent to the "likes" count. I focus more on the comments and questions.

Virtual Assistants

These are people working for you but are not based in your office. Are there any repetitive or non-income generating tasks that you could outsource to a highly qualified person in the Philippines for only $400-$500 a month, working full-time? Now don't feel bad about paying someone such a small amount of money—**that is a very highly paid wage** in the Philippines; they will be grateful for receiving so much money.

A number of my property-investing friends use a VA. They tend to use them for data scraping, programming, CRM systems, accounting, bookkeeping and outbound calls. Some have more than one VA.

You can hire a VA directly at:
upwork.com
Onlinejobs.ph

Or hire an agency with a team of employees:
taskbullet.com

Alternatively, you could employ an in-person Personal Assistant at your office. Many successful people started by hiring their mother.

Unwanted phone calls
If you are getting too many phone calls to manage, you could outsource the answering of your phone to alldaypa.co.uk in the UK. They can screen the calls and email you if there is anything important.

We got rid of our landline and only use mobile phones instead—this stopped nearly all of the junk calls about PPI and car accident claims.

People often ask for my phone number, and are slightly irritated when I say no. I get so many people contacting me, that we decided to removed our personal telephone number from our website and social media pages, and don't list them on any online or printed business directories anymore. We don't want to reach to the point where we can't even accept calls from our mothers, due to the volume of calls.

Sarah changed her voicemail to tell people that she never checks her voicemail for messages—to email instead. She is not always in a position to answer her phone whilst driving or looking after the children, so she doesn't pick it up. If people really want to get hold of her, they will email.

Calendar
Sarah previously managed her life in a paper diary, and I used an online calendar. We found that we were constantly doubling up on work, by duplicating each other's schedule in our diaries. It could take 30-60 minutes for us to coordinate.

Eventually I managed to convince Sarah to share my calendar in iCal. This means we can both view our combined diary on our iPhones and Mac computers. We have colour coded the entries for George only, Sarah only, Both, and our Kids. There are plenty of other online calendar options to choose from, so chose one you can all access from your phones and desktop computer.

We put in all repeating diary items such as the gym, refuse collection and anniversaries as automated recurring entries—so we only need to do it once.

We put our "To do" items as all day events, and then delete them when they are done.

Now we know what the other one is doing each day…and slightly more dangerously, we can assign each other tasks!

Every Monday morning at 5am, we discuss the week ahead, so we both know what's going on and can keep aligned.

Chunking
Remember that time when you had that really bad night out drinking alcohol…and then chased it down with a kebab…

…no this is nothing to do with vomit!

It's about spending a concentrated amount of time on only one task, rather than scattering it throughout the week. It can take time for your brain to get into flow, so it's a lot easier to do the whole job in one go.

If you do your own bookkeeping, batch it to once a week, or once a month. Alternatively, you could outsource to a VA in the UK or overseas.

Email

I recommend you close your email program while you are working on a key task. It gets really distracting when you see the little red numbers increasing while you are doing something on the computer. Your eyes keep looking at it and thinking "I really need to check what that is" and it stops the flow of the task at hand.

Therefore, whenever I'm working on something, such as writing this book, analysing a property, or sitting back and brainstorming on our business or my personal development, I close my email program and social media, so that I don't see the notifications. I probably spend more time with the email program closed, rather than launched.

You could also decide to chunk emails. If you email one of our friends, you will receive an auto responder email stating that she only checks her emails twice a day at certain times. That's something you could consider doing—you don't have to send out a message, you could just allocate the times to the task.

Unsubscribe—every time I get an email that I'm not interested in, I unsubscribe. Because if you keep pressing delete, and they are emailing you every day, then that's 365 decisions you've had to make over a year. Each time you make a decision, you fatigue yourself.

Mouse speed

If you go into your computer's system preferences, you

can change the tracking speed. Instead of having to pick the mouse up to scroll from one side of the screen to the other, you can increase the tracking speed to make the mouse more sensitive—now you barely need to physically move it. This takes a bit of getting used to, so you might need to gradually increase it once a day until you get to the fastest setting.

Once you get used to it, then everyone else's computer seems really s l o w!

Find your best time to work
In the book *When: The Scientific Secrets of Perfect Timing* by Daniel H. Pink, he demonstrates that there is a best time of day for the type of task at hand.
mycastleproperty.co.uk/whenpink

You might be a Lark, Owl or somewhere in-between (Third Birds). You probably already have a good idea of what time of day you are most productive. For Sarah and I that is early morning—we currently rise at 5am and get a few things done before our two children wake up at 6am. We also meditate and read a book. If I need to do anything analytical, that's the best time for me as there are fewer distractions. If you're a night owl, then do those key tasks when you feel your peak in the evening.

Conversely, it's useful for me to do the more mundane administration tasks in the afternoon—when I don't have to concentrate that much. The afternoon is also a good time for me to brainstorm.

I'm not too much a stickler for scheduling things at the right time, except to put one task in the morning that requires my full attention.

The other key takeaway from Pink's book is to take restorative breaks. In today's society, it seems the norm to sit at your desk all day, eat lunch at your desk, and not hang around the coffee machine.

However, your brain can't focus for 7 hours straight. You become less productive and easily distracted.

Think of breaks as a way to increase your efficiency. Take a real lunch break. Try to get out of the office—ideally with a friend—and don't talk about work.

Have a 15 to 20-minute restorative coffee break in the mid-morning and mid-afternoon. You will feel better for it. Maybe go for a walk, to get the blood stirring.

In addition, I know a number of successful people who practice *The Miracle Morning*, a productivity book by Hal Elrod. They spend the first hour of the day with meditation, exercise and reading…so they can "level up" their lives.

"Clutter represents indecisions" — Marie Kondo

Physical or electronic clutter on your computer will slow you down and erode your decision-making willpower.

The last time we moved, we went through our entire possessions and sold or gave away anything we hadn't used for six months. It was emotionally draining, as it fatigued our decision bank.

We started with easy items such as clothes and books. We emptied the loft into our garden after we'd gone through every room—that was a complete nightmare to go through! We managed to reduce our possessions by about 40%.

We also set up archive folders for our emails and deleted some of the files on our network storage.

Decision fatigue
We are bombarded by decisions to make, every second of the day. There are emails to action, social media notifications, text messages, post in the mail, deciding what to eat, what to wear…

Decision fatigue hits your willpower bank and can make you irritable and even angry. By automating as much as you can in your life, so you don't need to choose anymore, you can improve your happiness.

Simplify—if you cut down the number of decisions that you need to make, you will feel less tired and can focus on the decisions that really count.

Many successful people wear the same outfit every day.

Steve Jobs wore a black turtleneck and blue jeans, and Mark Zuckerberg wears a grey t-shirt and blue jeans. Moreover, if you could cut down your wardrobe a little, you will feel uplifted and won't spend time deliberating over what to wear today. It will also save you money and time shopping.

I remember when I was a Personal Trainer, I wore the same branded jogging bottoms and vest every day. It was quite a relief to put on my uniform every morning, as I didn't have to think. I haven't gone back to those days, but I currently only have about 10 days of tops, clones of underwear and socks, and only two pairs of trainers.

Bookkeeping
Previously we had box files of receipts and were logging entries in Excel. When we were emailed a receipt, we would print it out for the files. We had so much paperwork, that went into cardboard boxes and were put in the loft each year…never to be seen again. It wasn't very eco-friendly, or time efficient.

Now we use the online bookkeeping and accounting software Xero. It automatically feeds in our bank transactions and recognises regular payments or credits—so reconciling the accounts is a doddle. It even tells you "good job" when you are reconciled—it's like receiving a high-five.

Our Accountant can also directly access our Xero accounts, which makes it easy for her to change any setups, and to produce our annual accounts.

At the time of publishing, it only cost £11 a month, per company for the basic Xero package. It has massively reduced the amount of time we spend bookkeeping, which can be done in less than one hour a month.

We don't print receipts anymore—we upload them electronically to Xero. We also try as much as possible not to print anything, so we can do our little bit to save the planet.

A lot of our property friends use Xero, and just as many use QuickBooks. Take a look at both and decide for yourself.

Cloud Storage
If you move all your data to the cloud, then wherever you are in the world you can access information from a computer or your phone—you can live the "laptop lifestyle." It has been really useful when we are on holiday.

If there are two or more people in your office then this is where it really shines, as you can access each other's files. You can also restrict which folders they can access.

There are many cloud storage providers out there, such as: Box, Google Drive, Microsoft OneDrive, Dropbox.

Choose one that fits your requirements and budget.

> You can watch a video on our Laptop Lifestyle in the RETIRE NOW! bonus resources page at mycastleproperty.co.uk/retirenowbonus

Learn to say "No"
This can be difficult. If someone is asking for your time, and there isn't an upside for you, then it could be time to say "no". The upside doesn't necessarily need to be money; for example, it could be meeting a more successful person, raising your profile in the industry, gaining knowledge, deals, or access to funds. Time becomes more valuable, the more successful you become…so spend it wisely!

There are greater numbers of people contacting us every day, asking questions about property, or to meet with them. And as time is the one thing most precious to Sarah and I—we are having to turn down more and more people every day.

Can I ask you for a favour? If you have a property or financial freedom question, please post it in our Facebook group *My Castle Property community*. We do check it regularly and will respond to questions.

Think about your Dream Board—does the request for your time conflict with it? Do you say "arrgh" when you think about it? If so, then it is your cue to decline; particularly if you don't enjoy it and it will cost you money to travel and volunteer your time.

Give up the news

75% of the content in Newspapers and TV is negative news—take a good look next time and you will see that bad news sells. You spend your whole day worrying about things and feeling depressed. Take Brexit for example, you probably thought about it multiple times a day. What about that awful disaster in xyz? What about that showbiz celebrity?

Would you willingly opt in to receive multiple letters each day about these topics? No. Then don't allow them to spam you with depressing content.

Since we stopped watching the news, we have heard of many other successful people confirming they avoid it, such as Tim Ferris, author of the *The 4-Hour Work Week*.

Instead, we subscribe to specific topics or industry newsletters that we are interested in, and only digest them once a week. They are filtering the content for us. Just skim the headlines and only read the important or interesting information.

If something is really important, someone will tell you about it.

Spend the time you're saving on personal development, your business, or spending time with loved ones.

So, **rip off the Band-Aid and go on an immediate**

media fast for a week. See how much better mood you are in by the end of it. You'll save a ton of time anyway.

Exercise 27:
>Update your 7-day action plan with any systemisation tasks you will implement this week.

CHAPTER EIGHT
Education

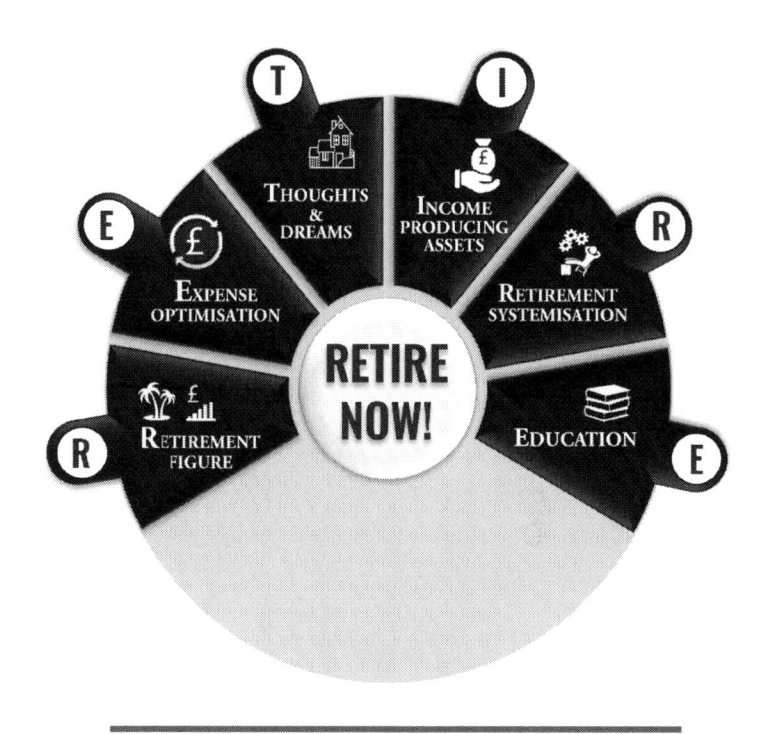

> "Leaders are readers"
>
> –JIM ROHN

Warren Buffett reads for five to six hours a day. Elon

Musk reportedly read for ten hours a day when he was a child. According to an interview in Time Magazine, Bill Gates reads fifty books a year. Reportedly most CEOs read one book a week. How about you?

To make your property business more successful, you need to continually educate yourself. And if you just implement one tip from a course, seminar or book, it could save or make you thousands of pounds. As your property portfolio gets larger, these tweaks can grow into hundreds and thousands of pounds.

We like to read about property, businesses, efficiency, mindset, health and fitness. What would help you?

How to consume more books

You can use NETime (No Extra Time)—there are plenty of opportunities where you could learn whilst you are doing something else, such as reading whilst on a train, or listening to an audio book or podcast whilst driving or walking to work.

There's a huge selection of audio books at audible.co.uk and you can increase the playing speed to consume them faster.

You could also learn how to speed-read. We occasionally run a course teaching people how to double or triple their reading speed…so imagine how many more books you could read in your lifetime. I can speed read a physical book in much less time than the fastest speed I can listen to, so my preferred choice is always a physical book.

Or you could read a book summary before buying it. For example, Blinkist summarises a book in fifteen minutes.

Learn "Just in time." You are more likely to retain information in your long-term memory when you are just about to implement it—try not to read them months before you are going to do it.

Moreover, if you've signed up for multiple property courses, then perhaps don't take all of them at once. Just pick one course and implement that strategy…then move to the next one.

Property Courses
There are many providers to choose from. They all have different styles and courses. Some have more high-pressure selling tactics than others. Investigate them thoroughly and decide which ones meet your needs and you feel comfortable with.

Some that you will come across are:
- Touchstone Education
- Property Investors Network
- Progressive Property
- Samuel Leeds

Many of them also have free introductory courses, so you can get to know them better.

Trade journals

There are a number of useful magazines, such as:
- YPN Magazine
- Property Investor News
- NLA or RLA members magazine—aimed at the BTL strategy. The two organisations are merging to create the NRLA.

YPN magazine also has a huge archive that you can access online once you've subscribed.

Podcasts and YouTube

Many of the journals and education providers also have their own channels.

When I was just starting to think about SA, I found *The Serviced Accommodation Podcast* by Chris and Ritchie was really useful.

For business and personal development, I like to listen to the Tony Robbins and Tim Ferris podcasts, as they interview world-class performers covering every topic you can imagine.

Blogs

There are plenty of people out there with blogs or video logs (vlogs). Sarah and I produce a weekly vlog *Diary of a Property Investor* at mycastleproperty.co.uk, where we tell you what we've been up to in property that week—good and bad—and we share our learnings with you.

> "The more you learn, the more you earn."
>
> —Warren Buffett

Earn and Learn

Perhaps you've already attended a property course, or read a book…but you're still unsure, and want to learn more about how to actually do it in practice.

What you could do, is to lend money to a property investor experienced in the strategy you are interested in—and in return, you receive a high level of interest (Earn) and the opportunity to Learn by being involved.

In effect you are getting paid to learn—how crazy is that! I once did this on a large development. Firstly, I attended a commercial to residential conversion course, but I was a little nervous about implementing it on such a large scale.

We hadn't found a deal that met our investment criteria and had £250,000 in savings burning a hole in our pocket—it was earning less than the 1.9% rate of inflation…we were losing money by the second!

So, we provided private finance to a development — the Whitby Engine Shed, working with Andrew Bartlett and Peter Abell.

RETIRE NOW!

The Whitby Engine Shed was built in 1847 and designed by GT Andrews. This Grade II listed building had fallen into disrepair in the past, and its future commercial viability was uncertain.

It was a car park when they purchased it, and it was sold with planning permission for nine luxury holiday apartments.

Upon buying the property they discovered that the end had been demolished during the war — it was possible to extend it, to add two further apartments, making eleven in total.

The unexpected side extension was the reason for the shortage of funding.

Many developments can take up to two years and we didn't want to tie up money for that amount of time. However, the Engine Shed was already a significant way through the build, so the finance would be back out in a couple of months. That gave us time to look for our next property purchase in the meantime.

We also included a large amount of **learning components** into the agreement, including regular site visits, meetings with building contractor, and so on, to further develop our property knowledge.

You can see the stages of development of the Whitby Engine Shed and financials at:
mycastleproperty.co.uk/property-projects

Another way to learn for free (or get paid to learn) is to get a full-time or part-time job in a Lettings Agency, Commercial Agency, SA Management company, or a Property Training company. Or you could even volunteer to work for free in exchange for training.

> **"Your level of success will seldom exceed your level of personal development, because success is something you attract by the person you become."**
>
> –JIM ROHN

So, we stay on the path of continual learning, and love it! Don't restrict yourself to property. Think about business, health, mindset, and anything which will take you to the next level.

Exercise

How do you plan to learn more? E.g. read X minutes per day; listen to a podcast on the way to work; learn to speed read.

Decide what works for you and write it in your Action Plans.

CHAPTER NINE
Network

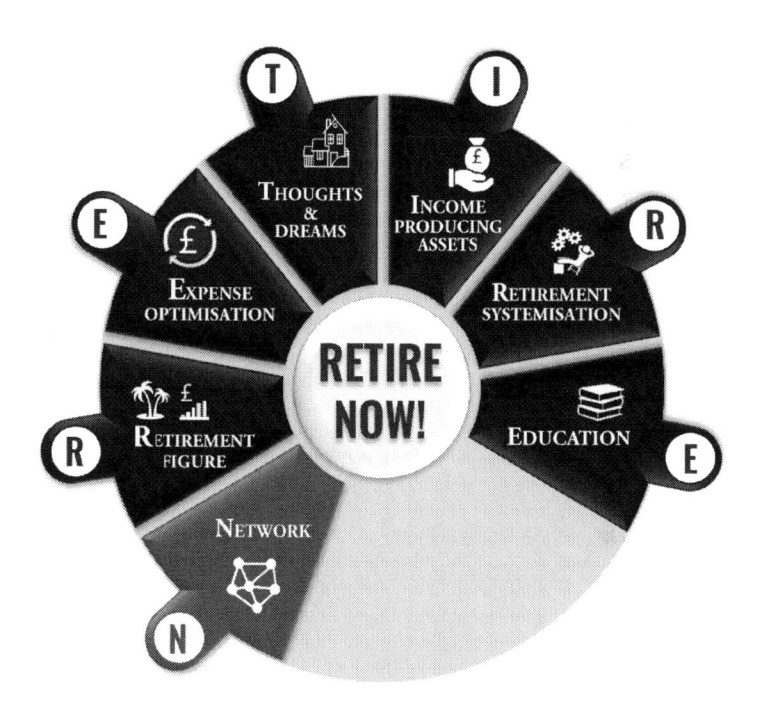

> **"Your Network is your Net Worth"**

I can't tell you how many times I've heard people say that

before. But I'd never truly believed it.

I'm very comfortable presenting on stage, or teaching—but if you put me in a crowded room of people like a nightclub, where I know absolutely nobody...it will be surprising to most people that I'm a bit of a shy wallflower! You'll find me just hiding awkwardly in the corner of the room.

Consequently, when I went to property networking meetings, I found them completely pointless. I only had superficial conversations with people, and they never ended up in any business ventures. I always left before the drinking started, as it was around my usual bedtime.

However, things changed when I joined a monthly mastermind programme. I developed a likeminded network of friends. It has enabled us to access people much more successful than us, who would have been beyond our reach in the past. It's a good idea to be the least successful person in the room—because if you do that, then your game will improve, and they will drag you up with them.

The difference between the property networking meetings I attended, and mastermind/mentoring, was the number of hours I spent with those people.

If you go to a networking meeting and only spend 15-30 minutes with a person, then you are never really getting to know them...never getting to build up any trust. It reportedly takes seven hours to build a relationship with someone. Therefore, if you are regularly meeting with your mentor or mastermind group each month, you will build a stronger network, more quickly. If you want to be a millionaire, hang out with millionaires.

I think I'd have got more out of the evening property networking meetings if I'd stayed for the after-meeting drinks until midnight…plenty of hours to get to know people. Unfortunately, that doesn't suit my "lark" circadian rhythms.

Also being involved in a Joint Venture (JV) gave me strong relationships, as I spent many days with them on site.

When you think about it, nearly every successful person has got a mentor or coach. People with no property seek out a millionaire for advice; millionaires seek out people with tens of millions; I know someone with hundreds of millions who has billionaires as mentors—most have multiple mentors. I sometimes meet people who think they "know it all". But as the billionaires are still actively learning from others, **I'm humble enough to know that the learning should never stop.**

Getting a mentor was something I'd resisted in the past—it all sounded too expensive. Why pay someone £600 or more per month for a one-day meeting? How could it give me that much value? All I can say is that I've gotten more out of having a mentor than its cost me—it has both saved me money, made me more money, and given me the fire to propel myself.

Making genuine relationships with relevant professionals (letting agents, residential agents, commercial surveyors, solicitors, accountants etc.) can make or break your property business. They can get you deals, give you free advice and ultimately save you lots of time and money.

We have saved ourselves thousands and avoided making costly mistakes just by asking a bit of timely advice from someone who knows more than us. You can reciprocate or pass the knowledge down to less experienced people—serving others.

Another relevant mindset is _Win:Win or no deal_. We only ever go into a deal if it mutually beneficial to all parties. It does not fit our values to take advantage of people, and if you do the same you can build up trust with your network which will make you more successful than getting a real bargain, but a bad reputation. That just isn't us.

In conclusion, if you work on building a meaningful property network, you'll be able to access knowledge, experience, funds and deals.

> "The shortest path to achievement, is to find someone already there."
>
> —GEORGE CHOY

Network

You are the sum of five people

Exercise 28: The five people

Write down the five people you spend the most hours with each week:
1. _Alan_ ✓
2. _John_
3. _Chelsea_
4. _Nat_
5. _____

You will become as successful as the average of those five people. Consequently, if they all talk negatively about property and think "it's too risky", or "the housing market is going to crash"—they will hold you back from becoming a success. And if they are poor, it will reduce your chances of becoming wealthy.

Try to replace them with new relationships—spend more time with successful and wealthy people. Don't wait, do it now.

Sarah and I went through this exercise many years ago, as most people didn't understand what we were doing in property. Apart from the time that we spend as a family, the people we now spend the greatest number of hours with each week are all property investors. We didn't do this all at once, we just slowly started spending less time with other people.

Online networks

It's also useful to participate in property groups on social media, so that you can get advice from others…and reciprocate by giving them help and encouragement to achieve their goals.

Exercise 29: Property groups

i) Go to the *My Castle Property community* on Facebook and leave a helpful message on one of the posts.

ii) What will you do to create valuable relationships? Hire a Mentor? Join a Mastermind? Set up an Earn and Learn? Decide what will work best for you and put it in your Action Plans.

CHAPTER TEN
One's Purpose

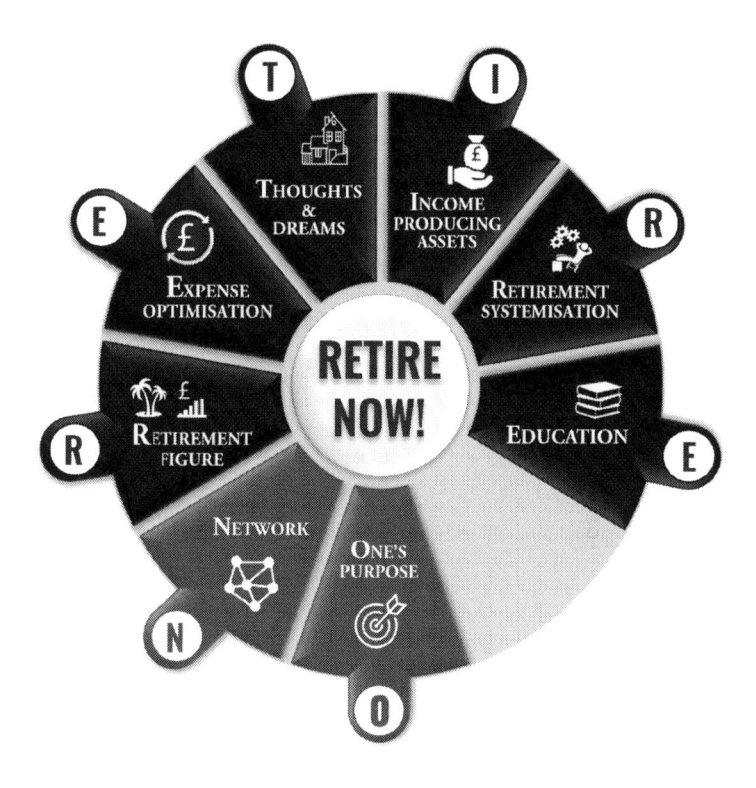

When we initially became financially free, we led a life of self-gratification. We spent our time at the spa, cinema, having days out and reading.

However, after six months our lives felt completely

empty—we felt like we didn't have a purpose. We wanted to give back and serve people, but we didn't know how.

In the past, Sarah and I have volunteered for things such as the children's schools, charities and community groups, but we weren't really enjoying them.

We decided to investigate some other charities…but couldn't really see anything that floated our boat. And after some of our previous mistakes with volunteering, we didn't want to sign up for something that we wouldn't look forward to.

We looked deep into our values. The top two subjects we always spoke about with our friends were also our top values—how to make people financially free through property; and how to improve your health and fitness.

According to Dr John Demartini, we should ask ourselves **"What would I absolutely love to do in life? And "How do I become handsomely or beautifully paid to do it?"**

We hadn't ever considered getting paid to live our values. Thus, you don't need to volunteer for free. One of my lifelong dreams was to become a lecturer when I retired. We enjoy chatting, mentoring and coaching people on property investing—so now we get paid for that instead. It also incentivises us to do it more often.

We do still go to the spa, cinema or have days out while

our children are at school. However, it's not all we do now, as we really enjoy mentoring and teaching.

Exercise 30: Getting paid for your Values

> Look at your Dream Board. Are your top three highest values on there? They should be.
>
> Can you think of a way that you could get paid to live your values? It doesn't need to be right now, but you can work towards it.

_____

_____

_____

_____

_____

_____

_____

_____

_____

_____

> Add it to your Dream Board and post your dream in the *My Castle Property community* on Facebook.

CHAPTER ELEVEN
Wellbeing

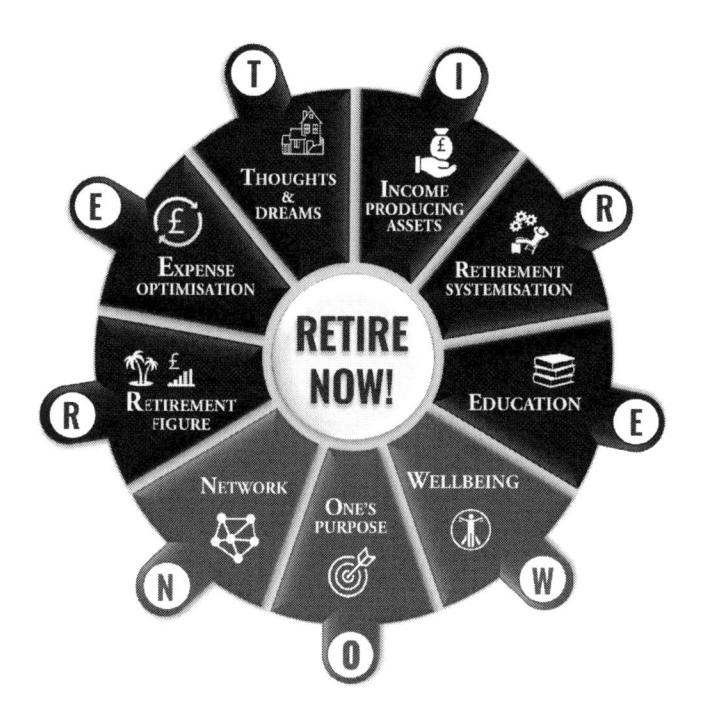

> "If you have no health, then you have no business"
>
> –GEORGE CHOY

My father was strong and athletic in his younger years. He got me into fitness. I remember trying to copy him doing push ups on our upstairs landing when I was only four years old. My father wasn't a large build, but he was incredibly strong. He carried a solid wood wardrobe on his back down two flights of stairs, all on his own.

At age sixty he realised he was a type II diabetic. At age sixty-five he was diagnosed with Parkinson's disease and my mother became his full-time carer. Very soon, my father found he couldn't walk, or even stand. He had to be strapped to a chair so that he wouldn't slide onto the floor. In the end he was almost a vegetable—he could barely speak. He got dementia, and sadly passed away with very little quality of life.

Take a look around at your friends and colleagues—it's not unusual to know someone in their fifties or sixties who either died or has been diagnosed with a serious medical condition.

What I like to do for myself is to use age sixty as a countdown clock for my possible demise. I want to hit age sixty in the best health possible, so I don't end up like my father. I aim to optimise my physical exercise and diet. How many years do you have left until you turn sixty? Or are you past it already?

The majority of people are dying from lifestyle diseases—this means **we all have complete control** over whether or not this happens to us—it is the food, drink and cigarettes you put in your mouths; it's the physical activity that you do or don't do. YOU get to choose your fate, and how long you have left to live.

According to a Public Health England report published in May 2017, 63.8% of adults in England are overweight.

Many people who are overweight, become diagnosed with type II diabetes. Many of those later contract Parkinson's. And some will also go on to get dementia. Therefore, there is a chain of events, that all starts with being overweight. So, if I can avoid becoming diabetic like my father, I can reduce my chances of suffering the same fate as him.

It's possible—like many people—that you've tried every diet under the sun over the years. Sarah and I have both been overweight and suffered with poor health in the past.

One day I looked at a photo of myself and I didn't like what I saw. I was 21 lbs overweight. My face looked so round. I was puffy.

I decided to qualify as a Personal Trainer, so that I could learn more about how to optimise my health and fitness.

I lost those 21 lbs, but I still had high blood pressure, high cholesterol, low testosterone, it took me a long time to recover from the gym, and **my heart would routinely stop for a fraction of a second** every day—I was only in my forties and felt like I was on the verge of dying. It was then that I realised that looking good, didn't always equal being healthy.

* * *

Sarah started at 56 lbs overweight. She had a lot of inflammation in her body, which created chronic pain. She had what felt like arthritis in her hand, and persistent constipation—which she'd suffered since the age of eighteen; she'd only go to the toilet once every couple of days, instead of daily. It seemed "normal" to her.

We took this journey together—she trained to be a Nutritional Consultant. We both got down to a healthy weight…but were not healthy inside.

Ninety five percent of people who lose weight will regain it after twelve months, because they don't know how to maintain it. They revert back to their previous lifestyle. We have kept to a healthy weight for over five years. So, we're not stick thin people that have looked good our whole lives. We've been fat and know how to shift the weight.

Our seven tips for health and longevity
1. Eat whole foods
Losing weight is really simple…

Eat fewer calories than you expend. Job done!

But don't starve, as your body will reduce its metabolism and burn less calories per day, leading to weight gain when you eat more again.

By far the easiest way to lose body fat without starving yourself is to only eat whole food. This means limiting or completely eliminating foods with multiple ingredients, that are packed with sugar, flour and fat.

For example, a chocolate muffin at a coffee shop, which is smaller than my fist, can amount to 450 to 500 calories. That is almost the same number of calories as an entire main meal!

Bread is a highly processed food with multiple ingredients. A lot of the nutrients have been taken out and even bleached. Each slice is relatively high calorie. Consequently, it raises your blood sugar very fast! It gives you a sugar high, followed by a massive crash.

Conversely, whole foods are those with only one ingredient. These natural foods contain less calories, and they are much more filling as they provide a lot of volume in the stomach. A sweet potato is only one ingredient, just as nature intended.

Simply switching to only whole food, is how we lost all of our weight. We didn't need to do any calorie counting— we just stopped when we were full or not hungry. We didn't do endless cardio either. We only went to the gym three times a week and did a little bit of walking in between.

However, there are some single ingredient foods that you should be more cautious about, such as those that are processed and refined. For example, a tablespoon of olive oil is devoid of the fibre and nutrients contained in raw olives. One tablespoon of oil is equal in calories to about 17 olives or a medium sweet potato. Which will fill you up more? It's easy to add a few tablespoons of oil when frying, but it's not good for your waistline.

Because of the calorie difference, we try not to use any pure oil in our food. Instead, we fry using water or vegetable stock—most people don't realise you can do that.

We are also very careful about how much peanut butter we use (versus eating peanuts). It's very easy to over consume peanut butter, as it is blended down, which increases the number of calories for the volume. There was a study that demonstrated that if you ate the same number of calories of nuts versus nut butters, your body will extract more calories from the nut butter. This is because some of the whole nuts will pass through you.

2. Eat a lot more fruit and vegetables

> "We should all be eating fruits and vegetables as if our lives depend on it—because they do."
>
> —Dr Michael Greger

We should all be eating at least 30 grams of fibre per day. However, the average person in the UK only eats 15 grams of fibre. This means that the vast majority of the UK population are constipated. Sarah was one of them. Be honest with yourself—do you go to the toilet at least once a day, every day?

What do you think is happening inside your body, if you are constipated? The waste from the food is in your system for longer and is building up toxins, which can lead to disease.

What can you do about it? Fruit and non-starchy

vegetables are very filling. They also contain very few calories for their size, as they are typically 80-90% water and contain fibre. They are packed with antioxidants, which counteract free radicals that are causing damage throughout the body.

The body likes to heal itself, given the right conditions.

Angina
In a 2001 study published in the Journal of the American Medical Association, Dr Dean Ornish reported a 91% reduction in angina attacks within a few weeks of putting patients on a diet that consisted only of plants (a.k.a. vegan diet).

High blood pressure
In a 2014 study in the journal *Nutrients*, Lap Tai and Sabaté found that vegetarians experienced 55% lower risks of hypertension, whereas, vegans reduced their risk by 75%.

In fact, after being a heavy meat eater for many years…when I begrudgingly switched to a 100% vegan diet to see what impact it had on my health, my blood pressure reduced by four levels, my heart problem disappeared, and my testosterone increased. I performed better in the gym, with an increased pump and faster recovery times. Sarah's constipation vanished and the pain in her hand disappeared.

If you're interested in trying a couple of vegan recipes,

then check out vetribe.com/home/vegan-recipes

3. Reduce meat and fat
Cancer
The World Health Organization has classified *processed meat* as "carcinogenic to humans." They state that it causes colorectal cancer.

The WHO states, "Examples of processed meat include hot dogs (frankfurters), ham, sausages, corned beef, and biltong or beef jerky as well as canned meat and meat-based preparations and sauces."

Unfortunately, I used to eat all of those by the bucketload in the old days…I'm trying to undo the damage now.

Would you willingly give your children a plate of cigarettes? They are also categorised as Class 1 carcinogens. If you wouldn't give cigarettes to children, then do your upmost to avoid eating processed meat yourself, and don't give it to your children.

Diabetes
Many people eat a low-carbohydrate diet, which is relatively high in fat, in order to reduce their risk of type-2 diabetes. We used to be one of them.

However, it bares thinking about how all those T2D medications get tested…those drug companies know how to induce diabetes in animals in order to test out new medications.

The first step in diabetes is becoming insulin resistant. So how do the drug companies do it? In "A practical guide for induction of type-2 diabetes" published in 2017 in Biomedicine & Pharmacotherapy, **they recommended you can successfully induce insulin resistance by feeding animals a high fat diet.** Therefore, it seems that the high-fat diet causes it—the high blood sugar is just a symptom, not the cause.

One of the biggest sources of fat in the diet, is saturated animal fat. Did you know that even for a lean meat such as chicken, 30% of the calories come from fat? I'm not picking on chicken, but just demonstrating that most people are eating more fat than they realise.

A 2018 study published in Annals of Nutrition and Metabolism compared meats and the occurrence of diabetes:
17 years of eating meat each week increased the risk of diabetes by 74%, compared with a vegetarian diet.

Consequently, consider eating a few meat-free meals per week to reduce your risk of diabetes.

4. Get enough sleep
It keeps you slim:
In a study of roughly 60,000 nurses over 16 years they compared sleeping 5 hours or less per night, versus 7 hours.

Those who slept 5 hours or less had 30% higher risk of gaining 30 lbs in bodyweight.

Sleep deprivation can increase energy intake by increasing the hormone ghrelin, which stimulates appetite. You probably notice this when you stay out late at a party…you get the "munchies." You naturally decrease your physical activity, as you feel more tired. Consequently, you eat more calories and burn less calories, leading to weight gain.

How do you avoid this predicament? I used to advise my Personal Training clients to take a 20-minute nap before a night out—so they could put some sleep in the bank. If they couldn't nap, then I asked them to be mindful of the hunger and realise that they weren't really hungry—it was just hormones.

Sleep isn't just good for the waistline. You will get sick less often and suffer from less depression or anxiety.

The World Health Organisation has classified nightshift working as a group two carcinogen—probably causing cancer.

Sometimes due to travel, illness, children, stress, or whatever, you might be way behind on your sleep. It's always a good idea to get up at the same time each day, because I find that sleeping in, just gives you a poor quality of sleep. Instead, go to bed a couple of hours earlier.

And don't be afraid to go to bed really early. I can remember many times when I've put my kids to bed at 6.30pm, and I could barely keep my eyes open whilst sitting on the sofa. Consequently, I've sent myself to bed, and slept all the way through to my alarm the next day.

There could be many reasons why your body is so tired—it could also be fighting off an infection.

The things I've found that worsen sleep the most are alcohol and drinking caffeine after lunchtime. Also, bright lights, or using devices with screens in the evening can delay the onset of sleep by forty minutes. I find working late will also do this, as the brain doesn't have time to relax. I need at least 1½ hours to wind down.

5. Strength training and mobility

Sarcopenia is a loss of muscle mass, which accelerates from the age of fifty years old. How old are you right now? If you're over fifty, have you noticed a decline yet? What steps are you taking to stem the tide?

The resulting loss of muscle mass will mean that activities of daily life like become difficult and eventually impossible. For example, getting out of a chair without holding on, getting up off the floor, walking ups stairs, or carrying shopping.

I'm close to turning fifty myself. Consequently, Sarah and I make strength building and mobility part of our weekly training—we're putting some strength in the bank for future years. Just 30-60 minutes in the gym three times a week, with heavy resistance, and some post workout stretching, is all you need.

If fact, I don't train to stay in the same condition that I'm in today. In every workout that I do, I aim to perform better than the workout before. That could be just one more rep, or slightly more resistance. So that means that every week, I am stronger than the week before…every year, I'm better than the year before.

I know that eventually my strength will decline. But I'm planning to have plenty in reserve, so that it will take a long time to come down.

6. Nature
Forests
The Japanese practice *Shinrin-yoku* (forest bathing) for preventative health care and healing. Simply sitting or walking in the woods for two hours, will stimulate your immune system. I know that I've felt wonderfully relaxed when I've stayed in properties surrounded by forest.

Sunshine
It improves your mood and reduces depression. It stimulates the natural production of vitamin D. It also improves your sleep, as it helps you to maintain a normal circadian rhythm.

In order to take advantage of vitamin D production, you only need 15 minutes in the summertime, with a lot of unprotected skin on show. In the winter, you will need a lot longer—alternatively you can take a vitamin D3 supplement, but it doesn't provide all the benefits of natural sunshine.

I used to sunbathe in my teens. But now I tend to get my 15 minutes in the sun, and then sit in the shade or inside. I only put on suntan lotion if I'm going to be out all day at a park, or some other activity. My aim is not to burn.

7. Support
You are the sum of the five people who you spend the most time with. So just like with property, if you hang

around with poor people, you will end up poor. If you hang around with overweight people, you will end up overweight too, as you subconsciously emulate their behaviours…and when you start losing weight, they will unknowingly try to sabotage your efforts, as you are disrupting their norm.

For example, one of my Personal Training clients recounted her visit to a friend's house. She had done a great job of losing a lot of weight. When she sat down, her friend put a huge pizza on the plate in front of her and asked her to eat it. My client felt obliged to eat it, as she had difficulty saying no to people.

Immediately after that, her friend thrust a bowl of ice cream into her hands and poured chocolates on top of it. Whether her friend realised it or not, her friend felt threatened by the success as it made her feel bad about herself. My clients recounted stories like this many times. It was usually their closest friends or partners. So be aware of it and be prepared to say no…or change your friends.

Instead, try to find active people who will support you and your health goals.

Also, meaningful relationships have been shown to influence your lifespan. For example, it is well documented that married men live longer.

You could also join healthy eating Facebook groups.

Exercise 31: Improving your health

What changes will you make to your health and fitness? Be specific. Write the steps you plan to take, and then put some on your Action Plans.

1. Eat whole foods
2. Eat a lot more fruit and vegetables
3. Reduce meat and fat
4. Get enough sleep
5. Strength training and mobility
6. Nature
7. Support

RETIRE NOW!

CHAPTER TWELVE

Property Investing—what would we have done differently?

We would have started much earlier. At the age of 16 I'd have set up my SSAS pension.

The opportunity provided by Airbnb and Booking.com wasn't around in those days, as the Internet was in its infancy and everyone was scared about shopping online. However, I'd have aimed to get my first Rent-to-Rent Serviced Accommodation unit at the age of 18.

Once I'd become Financially Independent from the income of a couple of R2Rs, I'd have quit my job to focus as a full-time property investor and work on expanding my knowledge.

> "Do not save what is left after spending, but spend what is left after saving."
>
> —WARREN BUFFETT

I would have bought a more sensible car for my first one, and stopped spending as much, so I could save for property. We'd have done the Expense Optimisation immediately, and been planning for retirement, even whilst living with my parents.

We would have curbed our spending and wouldn't have gone on so many holidays. We wasted a HUGE amount of money on cars, designer clothes and gadgets. Every car was worth at least one or two deposits on a house. Every holiday would have bought another house. Even today, £7,500 is enough to fund a deposit on a £50,000 house.

We would not have bought our first house. Instead we would've rented something small and purchased a Buy-To-Let. I would have acquired property in the north of England or parts of Scotland, as the returns were, and still are, much higher than the south—at least double the profitability. We might even have moved there.

I would have outsourced property management right from the beginning. I wouldn't have done any work on any property. Our only job should be to find and analyse the deal.

After we got a couple of BTLs going and had saved enough cash, we would have switched to Commercial Property—which is the main focus of our property strategy now.

We hope you enjoyed reading this book and become Financially Free sooner than you thought possible. **People who are willing to make sacrifices and take action**, can often become financially free in a year or less.

Remember, this sacrifice is only for short time. You'll have the rest of your life **to choose how you spend your days.** It's an amazing freedom to have.

So, take your Action Plans, go forth, and RETIRE NOW! Please do keep us updated in the *My Castle Property community* Facebook group—we'd love to read about your progress, and so would everyone else.

Live your dreams,

George & Sarah

We hope you enjoyed this book and have already taken steps to improve your life and your financial security.

We'd love it if you could please give us a five-star review on Amazon, so that we can rise up the bestsellers list and ultimately serve more people. The more people we can serve, the more lives we can free.

Thank you.

George & Sarah

Contact

For answers to property questions or financial freedom, please post in the *My Castle Property community* Facebook group.

If you're posting successes on your personal Facebook page, then use these hashtags as appropriate:
#retirenowblueprint
#liveyourdreams
People will be able to search for these hashtags and gain inspiration from them.

If you have a **correction or suggestion for the book**, please click on the *Submit Suggestion* button in the RETIRE NOW! Resources link:
mycastleproperty.co.uk/retirenowbonus

Training
We occasionally run property or personal development training that ties in with the book:
mycastleproperty.co.uk/training

Press, Media or Speaking enquiries
mycastleproperty.co.uk/contact

R to R Holiday Home for us?
Good yield Pg 133 →
Get 2 R to Rs.
iCal Calendar for me + Al to share
Calendar on phones.
Unsubscribe from emails
Change touching speed on mouse
When: The Scientific secrets of Perfect
timing Daniel Pink
7 day media fast!
YPN Magazine
Touchstone on line
The Serviced Accommodation Podcast.
Chris + Richie
Tony Robbins + Tim Ferris Podcasts
Win.Win. or no deal
My Castle Property Community + help on a post
Whole foods
No meat
Strength training + Stretches